DATE			

THE NEWS BUSINESS

John Chancellor
Walter R. Mears

THE NEWS
BUSINESS

HARPER & ROW, PUBLISHERS, New York
Cambridge, Philadelphia, San Francisco, London
Mexico City, São Paulo, Sydney

1817

FIRST EDITION
Designer: Sidney Feinberg

Library of Congress Cataloging in Publication Data

Chancellor, John, 1927 July 14–
    The news business.

    1. Journalism. I. Mears, Walter R., 1935–
II. Title.
PN4775.C48 1983   070.4′3   82–48126
ISBN 0–06–015104–8

---

83 84 85 86 87 10 9 8 7 6 5 4 3 2 1

Contents

THE NEWS BUSINESS

1 THE NEWS BUSINESS

THE break in the wooden guard rail is hard to see in the gray morning, as the rain slants across the ravine. Several cars pass over the bridge before a farmer in a pickup truck notices the broken rail and stops to look down.

The school bus is on its side, bright yellow against the green slope, its headlights on, its warning lights blinking. The farmer can hear the sound of children crying.

He passes the message to the state police on his citizens' band radio. It goes from there, by telephone, to hospitals. In a few minutes, the red lights of ambulances and police cars flash across the stubble of the harvested cornfields.

And so begins a news story. The school bus accident will join thousands of other events and occurrences on that day, part of a great river of information, carried by satellite links, high-speed teletypes and computerized word processors. The high-speed machines of the Associated Press transmit about 400,000 words a day, 1,000 stories every 24 hours.

Thirty miles from the scene of the school bus crash, a reporter at the city desk of a small Midwestern paper learns of the event while making his routine morning check with the state police. At the radio station across town, a broadcast reporter hears the news on the police radio frequency. Their reflexes are the same: find out what happened. At this point, they don't know much, only that a school bus has crashed and that children have died.

The radio station interrupts its disc jockey with a bulletin saying just that. Essential but cruel—no one knows yet who has survived and who has not. The newspaper reporter tells his editor. Reporters and photographers head for the scene and the hospital.

It is wrenching catastrophe for the town—and a story across the country. For those initial reporters relay word of the crash to the organizations that will tell the world of it. The newspaperman telephones the Associated Press bureau in Kansas City. The radio man calls United Press International. They are stringers, paid space rates to cover local stories for the wire services.

The story is developing. AP and UPI send their first, sketchy stories across the nation. Then come advisory notes:

"Editors: A reporter and photographer are en route to the scene of the school bus crash. There is as yet no word on the number of casualties."

At NBC News in New York, a copy clerk tears the copy from the printer and takes it to the editors. The producer in charge of national stories for *Nightly News* has just had his first sip of office coffee. The program is nine hours away, but there is work to be done right now. This is a story that will be prominent on the evening news, and he knows it.

He pulls out a map, looks for the closest NBC television affiliate, picks up the phone and calls the news director there. Crews are on the way, he's told, and some of the videotape they will shoot will be available in time for *Nightly News*. Next step: Call NBC Chicago, and order a network reporter and camera crew to the site of the crash. They'll charter a plane and be there in a couple of hours.

By now, the wire services have their own reporters and pho-

tographers on the road. They will be the first out-of-town reporters to get there; their bureaus are widely deployed, and
there's one close to almost any place a story breaks. There are
more than 120 Associated Press bureaus in the United States.

They'll check with the local stringers, get to the scene, talk
to the police, get the casualty list, telephone the details to the
bureau in Kansas City. The story is put together by editors
there, relayed to New York, then transmitted to newspapers
and broadcast stations that take the service.

When journalists talk about this, it is in a language as old as
the first telegraph lines. A story "moves" on the "wire." It may
be transmitted by way of a satellite, but the language of the
business is rooted in the days when telegraphers wearing green
eyeshades tapped out stories in Morse code, on wires that ran
along the railroad tracks.

Today the wire services, the great engines of newsgathering
and distribution, are at the center of the news business. The
wires provide both the text and the context of the news. In the
editor's office, on the telephone or in the conference room, every
daily news organization sorts and sifts the day's events to decide
what will be published or broadcast, how much space or time
it will get, and whether it belongs on the front page or back with
the classified ads.

AP and UPI are central to the process of decision. They are
the basic wire services. They deliver news, photos and radio
reports, at the local, state, national and international levels.
They cover the state governments and distribute stock market
tables and weather reports. The objective is to deliver everything an editor needs to put out a daily newspaper.

The Associated Press is the oldest and biggest, a cooperative
that in 1982 served about 1,350 daily newspapers and more
than 5,700 radio and television stations in the United States. It
is a nonprofit organization, owned by the newspapers it serves.
They aren't customers; they are members. In 1982, the AP
employed about 1,460 news and photo staffers.

United Press International is a privately owned company, with a news and photo staff of about 1,000. UPI says it has more than 1,000 newspaper clients. After losing money for years and changing ownership in 1982, it faces an uncertain future.

Each television news department—at NBC, ABC and CBS —employs over 1,000 news people, including technicians, and can call on help from several hundred radio affiliates and more than 200 television affiliates.

Although Reuters, the British news agency, has expanded its operations in the United States, and competes with the American wire services, it is strongest abroad and in international financial reporting.

New York wire supervisors control the wire. On the story of a school bus crash in the Midwest, they would be in frequent telephone contact with Kansas City as the story developed. It would belong on the daily news digest, the menu of major stories each wire service transmits to advise newspapers what is coming. There's a late-morning digest for newspapers that will be published the following morning, a midnight digest for afternoon newspapers.

In the trade, those are the "cycles," AMs and PMs. The evening news on television is, in effect, an AM operation, with access to the same stories that will be in the morning papers. The PMs' news cycle is comparable to that of breakfast time television programs.

The process of deciding what stories will be shown on television on any evening and published in AM newspapers the next day is one that begins at midmorning, Eastern time.

At 10:30 A.M., about a dozen people sit down in a fourth-floor conference room at the Associated Press Building, overlooking Rockefeller Plaza in New York, to talk about the day's news.

Across Manhattan at UPI headquarters, the process is more informal; no set meeting, but a series of discussions and telephone calls.

In Rockefeller Center, the staff of *NBC Nightly News,* about ten people, meets at 11:45 A.M.

There, and at like meetings in newsrooms across the country, editors have been assessing the day's events, the wire copy, the staff reporting, the stories assigned but yet to come. Now they begin planning the product, deciding what's important, what to do about it, and where to play it.

Editors must decide long before deadline which national and international stories belong on the front page, and at what length. The decision is subject to change, because the news doesn't stop, and what seems most important at noon may be forced further back in the paper by what happens at night.

The story of a school bus crash in the Midwest would be a subject of those conferences. It is a cold, impersonal process— the mathematics of the news business. If that crash killed two children, it would be a small story nationally. If it were twenty-two, it would be a major one.

Were that the case, the story would be at or near the top of AMs news digests moved by the wire services. It happened early in the day, on PMs time. But few afternoon papers in the East would be able to print more than the first sparse reports, scant on detail that would come later, after their deadlines.

News digests are agendas, and they are a factor in the decisions made in all newsrooms. The digests are brief summaries of the most important stories of the day—twelve, sometimes fourteen of them. They deliver the lead paragraph, and an editor can write a headline from them before the story arrives.

These digests are put together by editors who have been writing, editing and judging stories for years, and much of what they do is instinctive. Former Supreme Court Justice Potter Stewart once said that he could not define pornography, but knew it when he saw it. That's sometimes the way it is with news. The pros know it when they see it.

The story lineups assembled by the two wire services, and the story decisions at the networks and the newspapers, usually are similar and sometimes are almost identical.

That is the case simply because good, seasoned editors looking at the same set of events will come to many of the same conclusions. Some of those decisions are automatic. If the President is going to make an announcement on foreign policy at 3 P.M., that belongs on the digest, and the story about it belongs in the paper and on the air. If there is a major flood in the South, a government shake-up in the Middle East, those stories do too.

The more difficult calls come on another kind of story: the piece that is not of compelling importance today, but may be next month; or the investigative story; or the complex but potentially significant science story; or the politician who announces he wants to be President but nobody knows his name.

Decisions on stories like that are made every day, in every news organization. Some prove wrong; the information leads nowhere. Some are right, and because of them, American readers first learn that there is a city called Saigon, an office building named Watergate, a vaccine for polio or a would-be President named Jimmy Carter.

Then, too, there are stories that should be used because they are fun, or poignant, or odd. They aren't important, but it is important to find them and make space for them. All the news doesn't have to be bad, or momentous.

But much of it is. Like the school bus crash.

When the executive producer of *Nightly News* convenes his staff for their prenoon planning session, details of that disaster are on his desk.

It's the first story discussed, and at that hour, it looks to the producers and anchorman like the day's lead story. That will hinge in part on the pictures, which won't be seen in New York until later in the day. *Nightly News* is on the air for a half hour, but because of commercials, the news must be covered in twenty-two minutes. That's time for up to twenty stories, some of them covered in a few seconds, others in as much as five minutes.

The decision on the school bus story will wait. The rest of the program must be put together. In conference call, the *Nightly News* producers in the seven NBC domestic bureaus tell New York what they've got available. Those "offerings" range from a feature on West Coast computer programmers who live like hermits to the Washington bureau's plans for coverage of a presidential press conference.

When that's done, the executive producer, whose job is comparable to a managing editor's, goes over a list of offerings from NBC bureaus abroad. The news editor, who keeps track of all the day's stories, reports on what has happened so far and what is likely to happen later in the day.

After fifteen or twenty minutes together, the producers and the anchorman have a rough idea of what that evening's program will include. But there are more meetings to come.

Besides, no news summary, no conference, no digest lines, can guide the news; they can only follow it. All the planning was done, the promised stories set, at 4:09 on a snowy Washington afternoon in 1982, when a jetliner crashed into a Potomac River bridge. Suddenly the planning was insignificant, the editorial decisions didn't count. The story did.

At a morning newspaper and in network television, the pace accelerates as the day goes on. By 2 P.M. in New York, Europe is beginning to shut down, and Asia has been fast asleep for hours. Washington is generating its stories, at the midday briefings by White House and State Department spokesmen, in the debates and votes of a Congress that does much of its work late in the day or at night. The dynamics of public relations are at work too. Across the country, press agents have timed their releases, their client's speeches, their staged happenings, to take place in time for the evening TV news and the morning papers. In the age of television, presidential campaigns are shaped by the deadlines of the networks. Candidates want to be on the air.

That can work in reverse. Public relations people in a government agency or a corporation that has to acknowledge bad news

know that an announcement made at 5:30 on a Friday afternoon produces little coverage on television, and fewer newspapers are sold on Saturday than on other days. Federal government announcements that will affect financial markets are
issued after Wall Street has shut down at 4 P.M. White House
press agents choose the time of announcements according to the
way they hope to see the story played. If it makes the President
look good, it comes early, in time to be seen on television. If it
makes him look bad, it comes late.

As the day goes on, the wire services move news advisories,
messages to editors that supplement the news digests with late-
breaking stories. When major news is developing, they send
messages to editors, telling them what to expect and when.

By 3 P.M., it is decision time at *Nightly News.* There's another
conference, but this time it is limited to the executive producer,
his three deputies and the anchorman. It is a time for blunt talk
about the importance and quality of the stories available for the
evening's program. There are going to be some stories that will
be broadcast without pictures, written by the anchorman. Anchormen usually argue for those stories, and producers press to
get their videotape on the air.

So far, the producers haven't seen videotape on that school
bus accident, but it is coming later. They can take it in after the
program goes on the air, at 6:30 P.M. But the earlier the better.
Stories like the school bus crash generally arrive in New York
in the half hour before air time. The correspondent and crew
have had to fly from Chicago, cover the story, fly to an affiliated
station, edit the tape, write the narration, check the copy with
New York editors and, finally, send it to New York. After a day
like that, they're doing well to get it in on time—and many days
are like that.

At 3:30 P.M., there's a final meeting at *Nightly News.* The
lineup is set, and the executive producer announces it to his
staff. It includes the stories that are going to be covered, the
order in which they will be presented, and the exact amount of

air time the anchormen and the correspondents will get to tell them. They'll have to edit their own copy to fit the assigned time.

The school bus crash is going to be high in the program. Eleven children are dead; the driver and seven others are gravely injured. It will be covered in exactly one minute and forty-five seconds.

Not long after that last formal meeting at *Nightly News,* the editors of the New York *Times* hold their first formal meeting of the day. They've been at work on tomorrow's paper since midmorning. The foreign desk, the metropolitan desk, the national desk and the other departments have been preparing and updating "skeds," short for "schedule," meaning the stories they see coming. They make their cases for space for those stories. They get a hearing, no decisions yet.

There, as everywhere, the process involves some internal competition. At any newspaper, the city editor wants a piece by one of his reporters at the top of the front page. The editor who handles foreign copy argues that there is a better piece coming from Moscow, and it ought to be the lead. The editor who handles features wants front-page space for a story about the zoo.

By 5:15, when the newsroom at NBC is hectic, and getting more so, the senior editors of the *Times* are meeting to plan their front page.

The executive editor, the managing editor and their departmental editors discuss the stories ready or coming for tomorrow's *Times.* The *Times* man in Washington listens on a telephone hookup. When he has something to say, his words issue from a speaker in the ceiling in New York. *Times* voices often seem that way.

After about fifteen minutes, the discussion is done. The department editors go back to their desks, and the top editors decide what the front page is going to look like and what will be relegated to pages of lesser prominence. They do it by themselves because they want no further debate. They decide what will be out front in the *Times,* and they make a sketch of Page 1. In journalism, a page sketch like that is a "dummy."

So the decisions that shape the news most people read the next morning or see that evening are made within a few hours in the afternoon and early evening. The process is repeated, time zone to time zone, Boston *Globe* to Los Angeles *Times.*

There are nearly 1,400 afternoon newspapers—PMs—edited after midnight and in the morning, delivered to subscribers in the afternoon. Most of them are small or middle-sized newspapers which concentrate on local news, and few of them face direct competition.

They outnumber the morning newspapers by more than three to one. In 1982, there were 1,745 daily newspapers in the United States, fewer than 400 of them published in the morning.

But the flagship papers of American journalism, the biggest and most influential of the dailies, are morning newspapers. Among them are the New York *Times,* the Washington *Post,* the Chicago *Tribune,* and the Los Angeles *Times.*

Editorially, the AM has one insurmountable advantage: it can be an encyclopedia of the day before, because the news happens prior to its deadlines, from morning until midnight or later.

By noontime, and in most cases earlier than that, the afternoon newspaper is locked up for the day, although some have later editions and a PM on the West Coast can print news of what happened today on the East Coast because of the three-hour time difference. News from Europe and the Middle East breaks on PMs time. But those are exceptions. On most stories, the AMs get first crack because the clock is on their side. And the afternoon papers get their shot at the story the next day.

It happens every day, everywhere there is a newspaper or a broadcast news operation. The question always is the same:

What are we doing tomorrow. There may be a quick pat on the back for yesterday's story—or a rebuke for the one missed or misplayed. But that's secondary; tomorrow counts.

That's the simultaneous joy and torment of writing or editing news for a living. There's always another story, another edition, another broadcast. Yesterday's achievement won't last, but then neither will yesterday's lapse.

"As I look back over a misspent life," H. L. Mencken wrote, "I find myself more and more convinced that I had more fun doing news reporting than in any other enterprise. It really is the life of kings."

It certainly is the most enjoyable job in the business, but there is also satisfaction, and exhilaration, in laying out the evening newscast or the front page.

To critics of the news business, and there are many, there is something suspicious about the similarity of judgments reached in all those editorial conferences that shape competing products. They look at the result and see collusion, or conspiracy.

It is none of those. All news stories are not created equal. No newspaper can print all news stories. Just as the reporter must assign priorities in writing stories, the editor must assign priorities among stories.

An assortment of self-appointed monitors judges the product, most often from the right-wing perspective, and finds it wanting or worse. Journalists are accused of being pack reporters, of prying into the private lives of public officials in ways that keep good people out of government, of overreacting and underreacting, of being simplistic and of being suspiciously liberal.

The wire services serve newspapers with editorial philosophies that run from the left so far to the right that an AP story about taxpayers who cheat the government drew a complaint from an editor who argued that income taxes are wrong and the people who pay them are being cheated.

Lawrence A. Gobright was the AP's first Washington correspondent, and during the Civil War he described his assignment in words that apply today:

> My business is to communicate facts. My instructions do not allow me to make any comment upon the facts which I communicate. My dispatches are sent to papers of all manner of politics, and the editors say they are able to make their own comments upon the facts which are sent to them. I therefore confine myself to what I consider legitimate news. I do not act as a politician belonging to any school, but try to be truthful and impartial. My dispatches are merely dry matters of fact and detail. Some special correspondents may write to suit the temper of their organs. Although I try to write without regard to men and politics, I do not always escape censure.

No journalist does.

There are people who believe that journalists sit down at lunch or in secret conclave to decide what to write, then dutifully follow some sort of party line as to what is news and what is not.

Not so. The news business is among the most competitive of callings. Reporters spend their lives trying to produce the story the competition doesn't have. Editors strive to steer their reporters to that elusive goal. Publishers and producers want a product different from the one the other guy is delivering.

Years ago, a group of White House reporters, dissatisfied with the erratic nature of the questioning at presidential news conferences, got together to discuss coordination of the questions they would ask, so that a subject wouldn't be left hanging but would be thoroughly explored. They did so openly, and told the White House what they were doing. Two things happened: White House spokesmen said it was a cabal designed to make things more difficult for the President, and the reporters spent their whole meeting arguing with each other.

It wasn't attempted again.

Almost every day, one reporter succeeds in beating the other reporters on his assignment—and they go scrambling after the same story. The object becomes to get even and go one better, to find the new development that will beat the opposition the next day.

A lot of duplicated effort and wasted time goes into the competitive process. But the alternative is worse, for it is to suggest that whoever breaks the story owns the story. In the very process of hustling to catch up and get ahead next time, reporters discover new elements, different perspectives, fresh information.

Journalists make mistakes. Good journalists fix them, as quickly as possible, although the common—and valid—complaint is that the correction never shows up as prominently as the error.

But the errors that do get into print or onto the air are out there to be judged. Newspeople do not have the luxury enjoyed by many of those they cover. They can't get it wrong and then just slide off the subject.

When Ronald Reagan got his facts wrong, which wasn't unusual, his spokesmen argued that the point was valid even if the detail was flawed.

President Carter once gave an interview in which he said he had set a date for action by U.S. allies to punish Iran for holding the American hostages. He had not, and two days later, officials at the State Department, requesting anonymity, said that Carter had left a "misimpression" on the subject.

That wouldn't have been handled so gingerly if a reporter had written such a story in error, and tried to explain it the next day with another piece saying there had been a misimpression.

There is a rhythm to the news business as inevitable as the tides, and it becomes part of the nature of reporters and editors. It builds to every day's deadline, then begins building to the next.

While the evening's program is broadcast, the morning's newspaper printed, the next crew is coming to work to do it all again. They'll prepare stories tonight for tomorrow afternoon's newspapers, "overnight" stories.

At midnight, the wire services will move news digests for those newspapers, the breaking copy will be coming in from overseas, the early-morning news broadcasters will be racing to meet their deadlines.

And the whole cycle will begin again.

2 *LEADS*

EVERY story has to begin somewhere. This is about beginnings—what journalists call leads.

The lead is how you start, which sounds simple enough, except that it isn't. More wastebaskets have been filled with crumpled paper because of trouble with leads than anything else in newsrooms.

Leads are supposed to be brief, but not too brief. James Thurber once ran up against an editor who kept telling him the lead was too long. Finally, in frustration, he made it as brief as could be:

Dead.
That's what the man was when he was picked up.

It was a joke, of course. Thurber wrote too well to end a sentence with a preposition.

At the other extreme, some reporters who aren't kidding have tried to cram everything into a sentence. As in:

The mayor's office announced today that the federal government will provide $316,000, the state will contribute $223,000 and the city will put up $735,000 to finance summer job programs that should make employment available to 17,239 young people between June 15 and Sept. 5, mostly in public works projects.

That's so bad it's funny—but there are copy desks that inflict such writing upon readers.

Then, too, there are writers who wish they were poets. A little poetry goes a long way; too much chokes the lead. As in:

Jimmy Carter, the man who would be President, buckled on his political armor today and began his quest for the White House as a haze-shrouded sun rose over the magnolia trees in his small-town backyard.

It's easier to write bad leads than good ones.

Leads are the keynotes, the overtures, the tee shots of newswriting. Properly crafted, the lead answers questions before they are asked and promises more answers to follow. The lead sets the theme and points the way.

That is a lot to ask of a sentence or two. But it is neither so awesome nor so mysterious as it sounds. A lead is simply a disciplined beginning.

One of the highest compliments in journalism is to have it said that the writer got the lead right. No one gets it right every time; the selection of facts and the way in which they are packaged is too complex a task for perfection every time.

Getting it right means finding the phrase, the quotation or the fact that reaches the essence of the story.

Sometimes that is easy: a President is elected, a leader is dead, a war has ended. These stories are the exceptions. More commonly, there are competing sets of facts, all clamoring in the writer's mind to go first.

In January of 1981, a day came when two competing sets of facts arrived on the same day, and each one was important enough to have dominated the news for most of that month. On the day when Ronald Reagan was inaugurated President, the American hostages in Iran were released.

Those two events within one hour produced the biggest news day in a decade. For each of us, it meant combining the two stories into a single lead.

MEARS: I put the two stories together this way:
"WASHINGTON (AP)—Ronald Reagan became President of the United States on Tuesday, promising 'an era of national renewal' at home, and restraint but never surrender abroad, his inauguration blending the passage of power with a passage to freedom for 52 American hostages." We had to revise the story over the course of that afternoon and evening to cover the latest developments as the hostages headed West and Reagan took over the White House. We even inserted material that night and produced what in wire service language is called a "new lead," to cover the inaugural balls. I wish they were called dances. The note to editors explaining what was new in that last story said simply, "To update with balls." The hostage/ inauguration lead was difficult to handle. It wasn't complex, in that anyone had to choose among competing facts, since only two really counted. Reagan was President and the hostages were out. It was the combination of all this happening at the same time that we had worried about handling for weeks. It got to be a kind of in-house joke—what do we do if it all happens at once? So of course, it did.

CHANCELLOR: *Nightly News* had the same problem. We decided that the program would begin with Reagan taking the oath right at the very top, no announcer and no titles. But our first extended story was the hostage story. The reasoning behind that was that everyone had known since the previous November that Reagan would be inaugurated, but the hostages were not a predictable story, so we began with them. I wrote: "Good evening on the 444th and final day of the hostage crisis, which is also the first day of the new Reagan presidency." Then we went right to pictures of the hostages boarding the plane at Teheran airport. I did not know until I rolled the paper into the typewriter and sat there and said, What the hell am I going to write—and then all of a sudden it wrote itself. "Final" and "First" seemed to be the story to me.

MEARS: It took me a while to get the things into a manageable set of words. There was so much to cover and so few words to do it. I needed to say that Reagan had been inaugurated, I had to give some sense of his inaugural address, and I needed to cover the hostages. It would have been easy if he mentioned the hostages in the inaugural address, so of course he didn't. I struggled. Then I hit "passage of power—passage to freedom," which described both the combination and the contrast. After that it all fell into place. That's not unusual, in my experience; once you get a handle on the lead, and you're satisfied with it, the rest of the story usually comes easily.

CHANCELLOR: The biggest stories are usually the easiest to write. The Germans have surrendered. John Lennon has been killed by a maniac. The stock market lost forty points. The release of the hostages and the inauguration of Reagan were uncomplicated facts in themselves, which did blend into a coherent combination lead. Not all combinations are that way.

The best test to determine which competing fact gets top billing is to ask yourself: Which of the facts interests me most? Anyone who writes to inform must begin with more information than the reader or viewer. That rule seems obvious, but it isn't always observed. And a failure to recognize the most important among competing facts will produce a lead that runs away from responsibility, a lead that says the writer is lost.

Anytime you pick up the paper and read that the House has passed a complex tax bill, that story probably will tell you little. If it is too complex for the writer to explain in the lead, the story that follows will very likely be too complex to wade through.

There are differences between writing for newspapers and writing for television, but the fundamental obligation of the writer in either medium remains the same: get the essence of the story in the lead.

Choosing is the essence of leadwriting. Somewhere in any complicated story there are elements that lend themselves to simple, direct explanation. The job is to find them. A vague beginning usually means a vague story. The lead disciplines what comes afterward, and without that discipline, the succeeding paragraphs are likely to be aimless.

The easiest place to begin is the nice, simple, factual lead. Four men with guns held up the Amalgamated Bank on Main Street this morning and got away with $50,000.

CHANCELLOR: For radio and television, one does not write "four armed men," because the spoken phrase comes out as men with four arms—four-armed men. That lead would have to begin, "A strange band of men with four arms held up the Amalgamated Bank . . ." If there's a fact as bizarre as that, it belongs right up front. The strange band of four-armed men is more newsworthy than the robbery.

There is truth in the saying that the story tells itself. The writer's task is to get out of the way and write in plain, simple language what has happened. That can be done with style, and rhythm, and vivid phrasing. But it has to be done with simplicity too.

MEARS: When I look at stories written by college students, the lead very frequently will be something like: "The faculty committee met Wednesday." Period. The story goes on to say the committee decided something, and I say, Wait a minute, what the committee decided is the lead.

CHANCELLOR: The lead is: "From now on, students at Siwash will have to have their homework in on time." And then, in a second sentence, you tell how that decision was made, and that takes you to the meeting of the faculty committee.

MEARS: The committee could have decided a dozen things, but if the homework decision is the one that affects the people who'll be reading the story, that's the lead.

CHANCELLOR: I have a kind of rough rule. I sometimes pretend I'm calling my mother. I say to her, You know what they did here at Siwash? They say the students have to get their homework in on time. She might say, Who decided that? And I reply, the faculty committee. And that's the lead.

MEARS: What if you were forced to put it into a one-minute phone call—or less?

CHANCELLOR: If it takes one whole minute to say it or read it, you don't have a lead, you've got more than 125 words, and the worst editor in the world wouldn't let you put that lead in the paper. And if you're rattling off at that rate, you surely don't have it worked out in your head.

MEARS: I meant for that one-minute phone call to include some time for thinking. But I suppose you're right; that ought to be done before you get on the phone.

Working it out in your head makes it easier to avoid dressing up a lead with a word like "dramatic." If the event being described is dramatic, the word is unnecessary. If the event is not dramatic, writing that it is won't make it so.

Dramatic events produce such dreadful phrases as "emotional homecomings," "solemn vows" and "major speeches." "Homecoming" is an emotional word by itself. If vows aren't solemn, they don't count. No one ever admitted to making a minor speech. Writers are not salesmen for the events they recount. It is the description, not the shopworn adjective, that can make a lead extraordinary.

For example: Robert F. Kennedy is assassinated. Dramatic, ironic, tragic, shocking—all those words apply to what happened. But a lead can be fashioned without them: "Senator Robert F. Kennedy died of gunshot wounds early today, prey like his President brother to the savagery of an assassin." Writing that lead did not require a selection of facts. Writing that lead did require a selection of words. Using words like "dramatic" or "shocking" in that kind of lead is not only sloppy writing, it demeans the event itself.

Of course it was dramatic, and of course it was shocking. That's why it went without saying. That is not to say that it needed to be a lead without drama. But the drama is in the telling, as in the masterful lead with which Douglas B. Cornell of the AP told of the burial of Robert Kennedy.

> Robert F. Kennedy was buried on a gentle hillside Saturday in the uncertain light of a full moon and the flame flickering eternally over the grave of martyred President John F. Kennedy.

So, too, the day Richard M. Nixon resigned as President. The right lead was the simplest:

> Richard M. Nixon resigned today as the 37th President of the United States.

The reader comes soon enough to the fact that no President had ever resigned before. Say what happened and leave it alone.

CHANCELLOR: This is, perhaps, even more important in writing for television. Big news is very often bad news. Leads on these stories need to be spare and lean as possible. The viewer needs to know the facts, and needs a little time to let them soak in. It's one thing to pick up a newspaper, read of some calamity in the headline, and go on to read the story itself. It's another thing to watch a television news program. A reader can go at his own speed, but a viewer needs time to comprehend the news. Which is why I take my time with leads on really big stories, beginning with the basic fact, which just writes itself, then adding other facts as slowly and logically as I can. One way to help the viewer is to find a way to repeat the information contained in the first sentence in about the fourth or fifth ("Nixon's resignation became official as he was flying to California," not "It became official as . . ."). If it is done properly, the essential facts can be methodically outlined and reinforced in about half a minute of copy. And if you think that's a very short time, stop reading now, look at your watch, and think of the things you could say about a big story in thirty seconds.

Being simple does not mean being dull. Even in the most uncomplicated leads, there can be tension and vivid contrast. When the 1968 Democratic National Convention delivered its presidential nomination to Hubert H. Humphrey, there was discord in the convention hall, and rioting in downtown Chicago, where antiwar demonstrators battled police. It was a night of ironies—a gentle man reaching his life's goal in circumstances that belied everything he had preached in a long political career.

That could have been a "meanwhile" lead: Hubert H. Humphrey won the Democratic presidential nomination tonight. Meanwhile, there was rioting in downtown Chicago, a few miles from the convention hall.

"Meanwhile" leads are lousy leads. You can do anything with "meanwhile," but you'll usually regret it later. The stock market crashed today. Meanwhile, it snowed in Boise. "Meanwhile" is sometimes hard to avoid, and no one who writes can claim to be innocent of using it, but it is best left in the dictionary.

MEARS: My lead on the Humphrey nomination went this way: "Hubert H. Humphrey, apostle of the politics of joy, won the Democratic presidential nomination tonight under armed guard." That gets the Humphrey trademark, the nomination and the tumult of the Chicago rioting into a sentence. It doesn't refer specifically to the rioting, which comes in the second sentence, but it makes the point indirectly.

A lot of newswriting involves telling people something they already know. Between wire service bulletins broadcast on the radio and television network special reports which interrupt the soap operas, most people are going to know something big has happened. They hear it on their car radios, or other people tell them. Because of television, everyone gets to be something of an expert, and in many cases an eyewitness to breaking news. That makes more difficult the task of commanding attention in a lead. In many cases, the consumer is looking for confirmation and explanation of what is already known—possibly seen, live and in color.

Leadwriting becomes even more difficult when the story is not dominated by a single event, but describes an assortment of facts. That happens, for example, on a night of speechmaking at a political convention, or in a crisis which brings reaction— or response—from other countries, or when a President sends one of his major messages to Congress.

MEARS: One of the toughest annual stories to write is the President's budget message.

CHANCELLOR: Sometimes the budget doesn't produce an overriding lead, so I write what you might call an omnibus lead. It says the President has made his budget proposals, and then I list the most important ones. It takes a lot of words, and it's cumbersome.

MEARS: In my terms, that's not a lead. You've got to choose. For instance, you may have to say the dollar figure is the important one, even though to many people that is not a meaningful figure. Nobody in the damn world understands 900 billion dollars.

CHANCELLOR: It seems to me that one way of writing that lead is to find a shift in the way the White House proposes that money be spent. The lead might be that the President proposes spending more on defense, and less for the poor and the old.

MEARS: If that's in there, that's a lead.

CHANCELLOR: But suppose you've got four categories of that kind of change in the budget, and all are about equal in importance? You can't explain them all in the lead.

MEARS: Then you've got to pick one.

CHANCELLOR: Maybe *you*'ve got to pick one, but in television I can come on and say, in effect, Hello, the budget: Here's what they want to do to you and for you.

MEARS: I couldn't write that as a hard news lead.

There are some leads that seem to be repeated again and again. The President gives his State of the Union address. If he's a Republican, his party's leaders praise it, and Democratic leaders don't. The standard lead goes something like this: "Reaction to President Reagan's State of the Union address varied along party lines tonight, as Republicans applauded while Democrats complained that he ignored key social programs." With variations, that is written annually. Change the name, reverse the parties, insert different grounds for complaint, and the lead will stand up in the next administration. And it will be just as dull the next time.

There's a better way, and it is to find one or two politicians who said something that wasn't predictable, something fresh and quotable. When the story is predictable, just pick what's interesting. All politicians think they are interesting, and some of them occasionally are.

Not all stories are equally newsworthy. Sad to report, some aren't very newsworthy at all—yet some in that category are unavoidable. People do need to know about an annual report from the governor's office or the school board. It may not be exciting, but it goes with the territory. The job is to make it as interesting as possible. There is always—at least almost always —something buried in all those pages. Sometimes it takes quite a search, but it will be there and it will be the lead. Otherwise you'd wind up with copy that began: "The school board issued its annual report today and it was really dull." That's a good way to begin the search for another line of work.

It's likely that a beginning reporter is going to be assigned some of those predictable stories. They are like slices of bread in the toaster: They pop up at intervals. In a way they are drudge work, but they also are a challenge because it takes extra effort, observation and reporting to find the ingredients that make this year's story different—better—than the one in the file from last year.

The city council members are sworn in, or the groundhog sees his shadow, or school opens with more pupils, or fewer, than a year ago. That property tax increase enacted six months ago takes effect tomorrow. It's the Fourth of July and, just like last year and every year before, there's going to be a parade.

Stories like that are routine, predictable and obligatory. They can be written from the files, with slight variations year to year. Or they can be written with some flair, by a reporter who tries to look beyond the routine and see something just a bit different.

For example, George Washington's birthday used to be a big sale day in the Washington stores. There'd be lines of customers waiting for ten-dollar automobiles and the like. And there would be annual stories about the sales gimmicks. The stories were as predictable as the loss-leader bargains. But it was possible to change the fare, as in:

> WASHINGTON—That silver dollar George Washington is supposed to have thrown across the Rappahannock River might buy a brand-new typewriter today.

Holiday stories are predictable. Christmas doesn't change much from one year to the next, but it's always in the paper. Parade stories are like that, or circus-coming-to-town stories. But news is about change, not about sameness, so the challenge is to find what is different about this Christmas, or this parade, and write it.

Journalism is white-collar work, too often at blue-collar wages, and much of it is imprecise; that's why it defies fixed rules. But there are some things to keep in mind. One of them is the definition of news, which depends on who's doing the defining. Gerald Johnson, an editorial writer for the Baltimore *Sun* and a historian as well, once said: "News is what interests a good newspaperman." James Reston of the New York *Times* defined news as a chronicle of conflict and change.

People do need to know about changes that may affect them. They need to know about conflicts, at home and abroad, because that affects them too. John F. Kennedy once said that domestic issues can be troublesome, but foreign policy can kill you.

If it's interesting, if it tells of change, if it reports—or explains —conflict, you've probably got your lead. That's as true of stories about the city council as of reports about the Kremlin.

There is nothing more humbling than to sit down at a desk stacked with handouts—our word for press releases—or speech texts, and be forced to sort out all the verbiage and turn it into a story to meet a deadline. But there are few things more satisfying than the experience of wading through it all and finding a lead which gives coherence and structure to the whole uncoordinated mess of information. That involves not only the freedom to choose but the necessity of choice. A good journalist has the capacity for decision, even when it runs against the grain.

MEARS: At one of John F. Kennedy's early press conferences, I was just a cut above office boy in the Washington bureau, but there were two things he said that I thought were important. It was right after John Glenn's first orbital flight, and Kennedy said he thought it was super that Glenn had circled the earth. And he also said that if Nikita Khrushchev came to New York for the UN General Assembly, he would like to meet him. That would have been a summit conference. Our guys kept writing that Kennedy thought it was just wonderful that Glenn had circled the earth. But I said, Excuse me, sirs, but don't you think we ought to lead this story with the fact that Kennedy has just invited Khrushchev to a summit conference in New York? And they said, No, you've got to go with the flow of the news. Finally, I sat down, with a certain temerity, for I was the junior man in the place, to write a sidebar on the summit story. But they were right. The story that was printed the next day—not only the AP copy, but the *Times*, the Washington *Post*, UPI, everybody—was that Kennedy had hailed the hero John Glenn for orbiting the earth. And the invitation to Khrushchev was buried elsewhere. The reason was, the Glenn thing had been going on for days, and leads on that made the editors comfortable and the readers comfortable, and it was the guaranteed story that was going to get the play. I still don't think it was the news.

One kind of lead that can work well—although it has to be done with care lest it misfire—is the lead that plays off an adage or a cliché, slightly amended. It uses a familiar phrase in a new setting. So when Lyndon B. Johnson traveled to Independence, Missouri, to sign, in the company of Harry S. Truman, the bill that created Medicare, this was the lead the reporter wrote:

> President Johnson journeyed a thousand miles today to sign the bill beginning government medical care for the aged and share "this moment of triumph" with Harry S. Truman.

That played off the Chinese proverb that a journey of a thousand miles begins with a single step. Some deskman took a single step of his own to undo it. He checked the mileage and changed the lead to say that President Johnson had journeyed 996 miles.

Reporters talk with each other a lot about the stories they are covering, but the good ones make their own decisions, independently, about the leads they write and the way to tell the story.

This independence can be difficult, particularly in national political reporting or on any other story that draws a crowd of newspeople. Some of the reporters in the crowd will write safely, with the pack, emphasizing the same points, even writing similar leads. Seasoned reporters have been known to check the wire service leads to make sure their copy covers the same ground. That way, cocktails and dinner are not interrupted with a call from the editor, complaining that the copy doesn't cover the same ground the wires do.

Candidates, especially presidential candidates, usually say

the same things every day, and the reporters who trail them and write about them tend to develop a caste system based on seniority. Those who have been following the candidate longest become walking encyclopedias on what's been said and done in the past. Let Ronald Reagan say he wants to withdraw the Strategic Arms Limitation Treaty from the Senate, and these encyclopedists will argue that there is no news in that, because he said something similar in Dallas five months earlier.

Ignore that kind of talk, and don't let some other reporter's judgment alter your own. If you're beaten on a story, you'll have to catch up—but choosing your own angle isn't being beaten. You are not writing for people who have heard every word uttered by the candidate. If you've done your homework, you know what he said five months earlier. The basic point is that if it is interesting to you as a well-informed writer, it is likely to be interesting to a well-informed reader or viewer.

MEARS: I wrote a story on Reagan and the SALT treaty during the 1980 campaign. It was based on an AP interview, and it came at a time when President Carter was denouncing Reagan daily as some kind of warmonger. Carter kept citing his opposition to the treaty as evidence that Reagan would be dangerous in the White House. It was a point of dispute, of conflict, and therefore a natural lead. A day after it appeared, Carter was making speeches about the interview while Reagan's people were trying to play down what their man had said.

CHANCELLOR: I read your story and gave it a pass because Reagan had said it five months previously. Sorry about that.

MEARS: That was your loss, not mine. I think you were wrong on that one, but we've all got to follow our instincts. Some days they'll steer you the wrong way. I remember a day like that in 1964. Senator Barry

Goldwater was opening his campaign in the New
Hampshire presidential primary. He had a news
conference at which he talked about defense issues and
also about the assassination of President Kennedy, two
months earlier. Goldwater said that strategic missiles
were not reliable weapons, and that the only sound
defensive system would rely on manned bombers. He
was an Air Force reserve pilot and he'd been arguing
that way for years. It was old stuff. The Kennedy
assassination was the most sensitive subject a politician
could mention at the time. So when Goldwater
mentioned it, I figured I had my lead. It was that
Goldwater had accused President Johnson of joining a
leftist attack on American conservatives by saying that
an atmosphere of hate was behind the assassination. My
mistake. A reporter who hadn't seen or heard
Goldwater until that day led his story with the missile
comments. The Defense Department accused Goldwater
of damaging national security. Suddenly it was the
senator against the Pentagon, an instant conflict, and an
old story made new. The story I dictated wound up on
the spike.

Leads can do wondrous things. Richard M. Nixon never said
he had a secret plan to end the Vietnam war, but history will
record that he said it. What Nixon said, in the cafeteria of a
New Hampshire textile mill one winter day in 1968, was that
as President he would end the war in the Pacific, and win the
peace. But Nixon said he would not second-guess the Johnson
administration by explaining how.

There were two ways to handle the lead. One was to quote
what Nixon had said. The other was to paraphrase and charac-
terize it.

The straight quote is, usually, preferable. But that day a
rookie political reporter wrote that Nixon had said he had a

secret plan to end the war, and that is what's going to be in some history books.

MEARS: I stuck with the Nixon quote in the lead I wrote
      that day and got wiped out—everybody used the
      competition's story. You learn some things by losing.

You'll lose some, but you'll win many more by sticking with the quote. It gives you an unassailable lead, for it is what the man said. Too many writers opt for the paraphrase to save a word or two. But the quotation tells it better in almost all cases. In the depths of Watergate, Nixon said, "I am not a crook." That was the lead. Barry Goldwater's 1964 assertion that "extremism in the pursuit of liberty is no vice" was a clear lead. So was Gerald Ford's description of the situation when he replaced Nixon: "Our long national nightmare is over."

If a quotation is both apt and graceful, it makes a natural lead because lead sentences are themselves best written when they are easy on the tongue. Whether you're writing for broadcast or for print, it helps to read the lead aloud. If a lead can't be phrased in graceful spoken English, it is not a well-crafted lead. It must be easy to say, as well as easy to understand.

MEARS: If you can say it, the likelihood is that it will read
      well. If it takes two breaths to say it, find the period
      key and use it. Although I have to admit some of mine
      require one very deep breath. If it sounds awful, it will
      read that way too. But be careful when writing in the
      company of colleagues. Read softly and be prepared to
      be taunted as a writer who can't type without moving
      his lips.

CHANCELLOR: One of the most effective leads I ever wrote
      was on a study of dietary habits of the elderly poor. It
      read: "Poor people eat cat food." The second sentence
      told how that had been learned.

MEARS: On some stories the words themselves give a
   particular flavor and texture to the lead. When the
   American hostages were released from Iran I used
   Biblical words, Old Testament words: "deliverance"
   and "passage." I wrote that they had been released
   from "Iranian bondage." I don't read the Bible a lot.
   Those words just seemed to fit that day.

Writing leads for the ear, instead of the eye, often calls for
different techniques. The British Broadcasting Corporation
uses single words as signals on many of its radio broadcasts.
The announcer will read: "Politics. The Labour Party today
voted . . ." or: "Europe. The Commissioners of the European
Economic Community . . ." or: "Football. Tottenham Hotspur
last night defeated . . ."
   The utility of these brief signals is obvious. The listener is told
that the subject is being changed, and gets a brief idea of what
the new subject will be. The writer of broadcast news must
always be aware that he is competing for the listener's attention.

CHANCELLOR: One of the most common mistakes in radio
   newswriting is the lead in which a key fact is stated
   only once and not repeated. For example: "Bolivian
   police today reported that twenty-four American
   tourists were rushed to hospitals with stomach
   poisoning after a Fourth of July picnic at the American
   embassy. Doctors say all will recover." If you missed
   the first word, you're lost. Better to say, "Bolivian
   authorities say all will recover." That's not very flashy,
   but it helps a listener who is already digesting, if you
   will pardon that word, the fact that a couple of dozen
   Americans got sick at a picnic at their own embassy.
   Broadcast news needs constant reinforcement.

Beware of leads that are too dense, too overladen with facts.
Suppose the day's big story is that inflation is down but unemployment is high. Here's the way not to write it:

"The government announced today that the rate of inflation calculated on an annual basis had declined from 4.6 percent in May to 3.5 percent in June, while unemployment continued at a postwar high of 9.2 percent during the same month, with more than 890,000 people out of work."

No lead needs that many facts. That one groans and creaks under the weight of everything that's in the sentence. Better to write: "Inflation eased during June, but unemployment remained at a postwar high of 9.2 percent."

The other elements need to be in the story, but they shouldn't be crammed into the lead.

The better lead is brief and simple. It has the same elements, but without an overdose of numbers.

MEARS: Long leads are not a problem as long as they're clear. The Associated Press once considered a ratings system for leads. You got points for short leads and short words. I went home and dug out the ten stories for which I got the Pulitzer Prize and found they would have flunked. I called the people who were setting up the system and said, "I just wanted you to know I flunked." The plan was never put into effect. Brevity is not the primary goal. Clarity is. The old rule holds that the shorter the lead, the better. That's old enough to be forgotten. There are limits, but a 25- or 30-word lead is not necessarily better than one 35 or 40 words long. It needs to be simple and understandable, not necessarily short. If it's clear and looks too long, put a period in the middle and make it two sentences. A lot of editors will tell you two-sentence leads are against the rules. To hell with them.

CHANCELLOR: There are times when a lead just falls into your lap. When the French National Assembly voted to abolish the death penalty, I wrote: "The guillotine got the ax today in the French National Assembly." But there are times when you simply can't write a short

lead. I remember the story of a frustrated lover who
murdered his girl friend, cut off her head and mailed it
to a former admirer, cut off her toes and sent five to
the President of the United States and five to the
President of the Soviet Union. All you could do with
that one was to tell it just that way.

MEARS: One of our guys was saying that his favorite lead of
all time was: "The nude body of a headless red-haired
woman was found today . . ." This came out as a
funny lead on an awful story, but it wasn't intended to
be funny. You've got to be careful with words.

There are times when there is no final story, but a lead must
be written, nevertheless. An election has been held, but no
candidate has been declared a winner. A jury is still out. The
Boy Scouts are still lost. This kind of leadwriting calls for more
imagination than the straight it-happened-today hard news
lead, and yet the basic principle remains. If the election hasn't
been settled, write it that way, perhaps with some color thrown
in about the candidates waiting. A lead on a jury unable to
make up its mind can be dressed up with a phrase or two
describing the vigil in the courtroom, but the story is still that
no verdict has been reached. Something that hasn't happened
can be hard news. It's a cliché but it's a story when the wedding
doesn't happen because the bride never showed up. The old
newsroom line is about the reporter who didn't file a story
because the wedding never happened.

CHANCELLOR: There are times when you've got to write
what I call a hedge-your-bet lead. I remember being on
deadline in Jerusalem once, when President Carter and
Prime Minister Begin were meeting on the Middle East
peace talks. Israeli officials said that things had gone
well, but Carter's press secretary, Jody Powell, had
given an extremely gloomy briefing at the end of the

Carter-Begin talks. I had confirmed that view after his public briefing by talking with Powell in his hotel room. I then wrote a hard lead that things looked very dark, and I showed it to Judy Woodruff, our White House correspondent. She said, "I know these Carter people. I think they're conning us. I don't think it's as bad as it looks." So I changed my lead to say that members of the President's party were extremely pessimistic in contrast to some optimism on the Israeli side, and added that it seemed too early to say that Mr. Carter's mission to Israel had ended in failure. The next day Mr. Carter went to Cairo, and a few hours after he arrived, his mission was a success. I had been saved by the caution of a colleague, and while the lead I wrote had a lot of on-the-one-hand and on-the-other-hand in it, it was accurate. Sometimes you've got to hedge.

We have found that a way to write good leads is to think of them in advance—to frame the lead while the story is unfolding. This can be of crucial help on a fast-breaking story, a briefing or an announcement that comes right on a deadline. When you've got to run to a telephone to start dictating, or when you've got to go on camera and start talking, the one thing you really need is to have a lead in your head. It doesn't have to be fancy, but if you frame it properly, the rest of the story will flow from it in a natural and graceful way. And you can have that very special pleasure of knowing you got the lead right.

3 *WHERE YOU GO FROM THERE*

IT WOULD make life in the news business a lot simpler if we could report that it's all a piece of cake when the lead is done. It isn't. That first sentence is crucial, and if it is done right, the story is on the way. It has a head. Now it needs a body.

Any body won't do. If it gets too fat, people are going to become bored with all the words. It is possible to smother information in words that look impressive but say nothing. But if the body is too scrawny, readers will look in vain for the information the lead has promised them. A well-written lead makes commitments to the reader, and they have to be fulfilled. The lead makes a point, or perhaps several. The story proves them.

Look at it that way, and the lead will provide a road map for the story that follows. There is no guarantee against detours, but it does give the writer a way to discipline the copy. In copy written for print, the first sequence of paragraphs all can work that way. They should tersely describe elements of the story that will be elaborated upon later. But that elaboration, like everything the newsman does, is subject to the stricture that never varies: There's not as much space as the reporter thinks the story ought to get. For a story about the end of the world, you might get all the news space you want. But there wouldn't be anyone to read it. Lesser events draw word budgets of four hundred, maybe six hundred words. That isn't many.

The limits of space and the promises of the lead provide form as you write. And a story fashioned that way will have form for the reader.

MEARS: I've always had a quirk about the way to build a story. Some reporters can put together the bottom of the piece and then go back to the beginning. I never could. I have to have that first paragraph settled or my mind doesn't work—I can't see the rest. I'm even worse than that. I want the lead to be clean copy, no mistakes or crossed-out words. Nobody ever said neatness counts, but I like it that way. After the first few paragraphs, I don't mind using the X. Or the XXXXX, which is one of the handiest keys on the typewriter. Or the delete key on the CRT, or the VDT, or whatever name you use for the computer terminal on which most of us write these days.

Once I was trying to get a handle on a feature story and it wouldn't come. I'd write the dateline and half a sentence, then make a mistake, yank the paper out of the typewriter and throw it away. I was so wrapped up in repeating the process that I didn't notice a colleague picking all that crumpled paper out of the wastebasket. He smoothed it out and bound it with a cover sheet, entitling it "The Collected Works of Walter R. Mears." It ran thirty pages or so. I'd thrown away one piece of paper with a dateline on it and nothing else. I told him that was because there are pieces of paper in the world that you simply can't work with.

I still have the thing somewhere. It helps not to take yourself too seriously.

CHANCELLOR: I try to make a list of all the elements of a
   story, all the quotes, and if the wires disagree on the
   number of casualties in a disaster, or anything else, I
   put down which wire service has which numbers. Let's
   say it's the story of a series of tornadoes hitting several
   states, killing people and destroying houses. I put the
   important elements down on a yellow legal pad—what
   towns were struck, how many people were killed or
   hurt, quotes from the cops. This does two things:
   It means that when I start writing, I won't forget
   something important; and it lets me see the relationships
   between some of the elements in the story. If I don't
   write it down, I may forget that the winds hit on the
   hottest day of the year. By itself, the hottest day isn't
   important, but if you slide it in somewhere, it makes
   the plight of the victims, and the efforts of the rescuers,
   more understandable in human terms. As anchorman
   on *Nightly News,* I used my lists to make sure that
   what I wrote did not duplicate what the reporters had
   in their stories from the field.

As you try to unfold the story, the process that produced the
lead has to be repeated, paragraph after paragraph. It is a little
easier now, but not much. About the only thing that is really
easy to do at the typewriter is change the ribbon. And sometimes that gets in backward.

Every word and every fact is a choice.

The information that didn't make the first cut and become
the lead may belong in the second paragraph, or the third, or
the tenth. As soon as one decision is made, there has to be
another, all the way to the end.

There has to be a reason for each sentence. If there isn't, the
story probably would be better written without it.

Without conscious decisions on what to include, where to go
and why, a story can wind up reading as though it was written
by a committee, at its worst a committee that never had any

meetings. The sentences won't flow one to another. The paragraphs won't fit together. There'll be facts, but no style.

A news story has a plot that unfolds, one paragraph to the next. It goes somewhere, in a logical sequence. Or it should.

The object isn't to fill space—there already are too many words competing for too little space. When there is a reason for what is there and a reason for what is not, the odds improve that the result will be a clear story with an identifiable style.

As you work your way through the notebook, the speech text, the election returns, there is another set of tough choices to be made. That is deciding what to leave out altogether. There's no way a story can include everything the writer knows about the subject. He's got to know more than can possibly fit into the space available.

A reporter sitting down to write a news story has to have more information about the subject than he can put into five hundred words, or a thousand. The information that isn't used isn't wasted. When you write, you've got to be an expert on what you are writing about. If you're not, it will show.

That's not to suggest that reporters go through life with notebooks and heads full of information they won't write for fear of offending their sources or violating some unwritten code. People outside the business read such accusations, or hear them, and sometimes believe them. They're wrong. When you're a reporter with a story, and can prove it, you write it.

The process of discarding some elements to make room for others is a mysterious one to people who don't deal in news, and it often is suspect. It is an inexact science, for it hinges on the subjective judgment of the reporter and the editors. They'll make mistakes. But they are professionals, and their livelihood is at stake if they make too many.

CHANCELLOR: There also are technical reasons for some of the things that don't get used or said. In television and radio reporting, on programs where there is an anchor in the studio, it's quite often necessary for the reporter

in the field to omit what would be the lead sentence of
the story. That's because the person in the studio has to
have something to say. You can't have anchors saying,
"Something terrible happened in Oshkosh today. Here's
a report." Anchors have to read hard leads, with facts
and figures. For one thing, they need useful work.
Besides, in TV, reporters at the scene of a story have to
deliver their accounts before the program goes on the
air. The anchor has to make sure the copy that is
broadcast has the latest information, or the reaction the
reporter in the field couldn't get. That is what the
anchorperson does: pulls it all together. David Brinkley
got bored once and decided to change all this. He
started writing anchorman introductions with no facts
in them, such as "And in San Francisco, here's Frank
Bourgholtzer. . . ." David decided he could use his own
time on camera to better advantage doing other stories.
But it fouled up the system, and drove everybody
crazy, and in the end, he was persuaded to return to
the more standard style. The goal is to include what's
needed to tell the story, fully and fairly, and to drop
the rest.

MEARS: I've covered five presidential election campaigns,
and I'm often asked how it is possible to write about
them objectively when as a citizen I must have a
preference for one candidate over the other. It's
possible because I have been trained, and have trained
myself, not to let that be a factor in my work. In a
campaign, my job is to tell people—voters—everything
I can about the candidates who want their support. If I
can't do that fairly, I can't buy the groceries or pay the
rent. I know I'm doing the job properly when I get
complaints from each side that I must secretly favor
the other. I vote, like everybody else. But I don't say

how. When Senator Barry Goldwater ran for President in 1964, the more vehement among his supporters used to challenge us at every stop on the campaign. "Tell the truth for once," they kept shouting. Finally, a colleague faced down a little old lady in tennis shoes and said to her: "Madam, the truth is not in me." I don't know what she thought, but she stopped shouting.

CHANCELLOR: When Spiro Agnew was Vice-President in 1969 and was attacking the press and television, our critics were talking about how people like me composed our faces. We were accused of inserting left-wing bias into our reporting by raising our eyebrows, or smirking. I went home one night and tried this in front of the mirror. I got to laughing so hard it was impossible to go on with the exercise. I do not believe that political reporters—reporters who cover the candidates—are secretly either left- or right-wing. The wire services and the networks won't put up with obvious bias, and neither will most newspapers. There are a few with strong political leanings, and there are some corres-pondents who know what the boss likes. My wife says I have no politics, and I think that's true of most reporters. It is true, in my judgment, that people who spend their lives observing problems, reporters who began by covering the police beat, tend to believe in activist programs for solving problems. But all activists are not liberals, and all reporters are not Democrats. Right-wing groups have been trying for years to prove the existence of a leftist cabal in the press. It is just not there.

There's no question that including one set of facts and skip-ping another can slant the story that results. That's why it is essential to choose with care, and to be aware that an omission can be as significant as what does get written.

Let both sides argue their cases with equal prominence. Unless you're writing about cops and robbers, there can't be good guys and bad guys.

That balance is particularly essential in stories about politics and politicians. There is always the danger of letting one side get the upper hand in a story because its exponents say things that are colorful or even outrageous.

The late Senator Joseph R. McCarthy made himself famous that way. In his Communist-hunting days, he would level an unsubstantiated charge late in the day, knowing that it would grab space and attention. Once, asked why he did it, McCarthy said it was because he knew "the boys"—which is what senators used to call reporters in another era—needed a story for the next afternoon's paper. There's no better way to grab space, in print or on the air, than to offer a fresh angle at an hour when there isn't much happening. That's the market McCarthy often tapped. He knew that when reporters for afternoon papers got his rhetoric and charges late in the day, they would most likely wind up as the lead on stories written for the next day's editions.

With variations, that technique is still in use. A politician or a public relations man bent on getting his story told and wise to the way things work will put it out for overnight use, or issue it for publication on a Monday. Not much happens on Sunday, so there's less competition for news space.

But there is competition always, among stories and among the elements that make up any story. There are judgment calls to be made, but there is always one imperative. The lead has to be backed up, substantiated and explained. It can't just hang there as an assertion. It's shorthand, and it demands elaboration.

Once the story says who won or who lost, who claimed or said what, the commitment has been made to report how and how much, to let the claimant try to back up his assertions, or give the full quote that wouldn't fit in the lead.

Republicans claim that they can heal the economy by reversing the Democrats' economic formula and cutting taxes in a time of inflation. The lead says what they promise. The story has to say how it is supposed to work.

That has always been so, even as the style and conventions of newswriting have changed. When the Norfolk *Virginian-Pilot* broke one of the momentous stories of the twentieth century, it was with a simple lead that stated what had happened and with subsequent paragraphs that told how. Here is part of the story of December 18, 1903:

> The problem of aerial navigation without the use of a balloon has been solved at last.
>
> Over the sand hills of the North Carolina coast yesterday, near Kitty Hawk, two Ohio men proved that they could soar through the air in a flying machine of their own construction, with the power to steer and speed it at will. . . .
>
> Like a monster bird, the invention hovered above the breakers and circled over the rolling sand hills at the command of its navigator and, after soaring for three miles, it gracefully descended to earth again and rested lightly upon the spot selected by the man in the car as a suitable landing place. . . .
>
> Wilbur and Orville Wright, two brothers, natives of Dayton, Ohio, have quietly, even secretly, perfected their invention and put it to a successful test. . . .
>
> The idea of the box kite has been adhered to strictly in the basic formation of the flying machine. A huge framework of light timbers, 33 feet wide, 5 feet deep and 5 feet across the box, forms the machine proper. This is covered with a tough, but light canvas.
>
> In the center, and suspended just below the bottom plane, is the small gasoline engine which furnished the motive power. . . . There are two six-bladed propellers.

That was written eighty years ago, in a style that wouldn't get past the copy desk today. But it met the basic test: The reporter told what had occurred and then explained the how and why.

That's true of any news story, or should be. Before you write too far, you've got to go back to the subject of the lead and fill it out with details.

MEARS: Once in a while it's going to be hard to do all that, no matter how much experience you've got. That's okay, it teaches humility.

In 1971, President Nixon announced that he was going to what we then called Communist China. It was in a television speech from Burbank, California. The White House said he'd speak to the nation on TV, but we didn't have a clue as to what he'd say. That's extraordinary; they really kept the lid on. We'd been trading insults and sometimes warring with China for twenty-two years. It's hard to imagine now what an incredible break with prior policy that was.

So Nixon goes on the tube and says he is going to pay a visit to the country whose leaders he has spent his whole career denouncing. Normally you'd have the files out. You'd know how long it had been since the Communists took over the mainland. You'd have some quotes from Nixon's political past. But this was a total surprise, and Nixon was on the air less than five minutes. I wrote the story, and it read this way:

LOS ANGELES (AP)—President Nixon announced Thursday night he will visit Communist China before next May at the invitation of Premier Chou En-lai.

We got that on the wire as a bulletin while I kept writing. "Nixon, speaking from nearby Burbank, Calif., said the visit was arranged during conferences between Chou and Dr. Henry A. Kissinger, White House adviser on national security affairs, from July 9 to 11.

"Nixon said he will undertake the trip 'as a journey for peace,

WHERE YOU GO FROM THERE

peace not only for this generation but for future generations on this earth.' "

I got two more paragraphs out of the announcement and I'd run out of things to write on what had to be the story of the year. Fortunately I had help, and the background that normally would have been there in the first story was available within a few minutes. It worked out. It also taught me something about writing on a subject you haven't studied. You can't just say, "The world is coming to an end next Tuesday," and then stop. People are entitled to know just a little more about it.

CHANCELLOR: When Nixon went off the air that day, I went on, to bring our presidential interlude to a close with some analysis. I was as flabbergasted as everybody else, and that was the first thing I said. It is important at times like that to share your ignorance with the audience. Hiding it can get you in terrible trouble. I did recall something about a "cold" Mr. Nixon's man Henry Kissinger had caught while on a trip to Pakistan a few weeks earlier. And I wondered, on the air, whether Kissinger's sniffles might have been a diplomatic excuse to cover his tracks while he was in Peking setting up the trip. That turned out to be accurate, and in this case, speculation didn't hurt the reporting.

Anytime the subject of a story doesn't like the story, he or she has a guaranteed comeback: It is out of context. In a way, that is always true. Everything is out of context, since there is neither the space nor the time to provide it in full. To put it into the kind of context some critics demand, you'd have to run a transcript of everything you cover. In the real world, the story has to provide its own context, as fully and accurately as possible.

Take President Eisenhower's celebrated comment that, given a week, he'd remember something Richard Nixon had decided as Vice-President.

That was in 1960, while Nixon was campaigning for President, saying that his time as Vice-President had given him practice and experience in the tasks of the presidency.

Ike made his comment at a news conference. It delighted the Democrats. Nixon supporters always claimed that Eisenhower would have had more to say on the subject, and would have taken the political sting out of the remark—but it was the last question.

Here's the sequence:

> *Q:* I just wondered if you could give us an example of a major idea of his that you had adopted in that role, as the decider and final—
>
> *Eisenhower:* If you give me a week, I might think of one. I don't remember.
>
> *Jack Bell (AP):* Thank you, Mr. President.

It never was clear whether Eisenhower really needed a week, or would have said more in behalf of his Vice-President. Time was up and the news conference was over. That was the context.

Here is the way that was reported in the New York *Times* the next day:

> WASHINGTON—President Eisenhower gave his own version today of Vice President Nixon's participation in administration foreign policy.
>
> The president told his news conference that he, and he alone, made the key executive decisions after consultation with his Cabinet, major aides and the vice president.
>
> Asked to give an example of a "major idea" put forth by Mr. Nixon that the president had subsequently adopted as a final governmental decision, Mr. Eisenhower responded:
>
> "If you give me a week, I might think of one. I don't remember."

That story, incidentally, made page 22, on August 25, 1960. In those days, presidential news conferences were held off camera—indeed, Eisenhower conducted them under rules which forbade the use of direct quotations until the White House had issued a text. All of that changed when John F. Kennedy began holding news conferences live on national television. Let any President since that time slight his Vice-President—particularly when the Vice-President is his party's presidential nominee—and it would not be far back in the paper or late in the evening's newscast. The White House news conference is a shared experience now, and anything said there is magnified by that fact.

MEARS: You know, in laying out a story, people who write for broadcast have a big edge on those of us who write for print. They get to say it first. By the time we can write it and get it printed, the surprise, or the shock, has worn off the information. It's news the next day, but it isn't new.

That has a big impact on the way we handle a story. It has to be done with some touches that don't come across on the air. It needs analysis and explanation that used to be left for the follow-ups. That's become more difficult during my career because TV and radio reporting has improved so greatly.

But if you can work some of those touches of explanation together with the facts—and write it with some style—you can deliver copy that will stand up through all the hours it takes to put it into the newspaper.

It's similar to what the news magazines try to do. They go in with the knowledge that a weekly magazine isn't going to break many stories that haven't been told before. So they rely on their reporters and writers to weave in color and explanation that will make what happened last week readable next week.

The kind of analytical touches I'm talking about

aren't those you find in a column or an editorial. It's a matter of filling in background, having enough information in your head or readily at hand so as to be able to say that today's announcement fits with these things that happened before.

The same holds for color, which means nothing more than saying what it looked like, or what the candidate did before he confessed, or how many people were on the floor when the Senate passed the bill. There's nothing very deep or significant about items like that, but they let the reader into the event in a special way.

We're always writing that the House today passed a bill to do such and such. What is too often missing is a description of how the House got to that point, how many people really had a hand in shaping the bill.

CHANCELLOR: One problem which affects us all is that once we've reported something, we think people are going to remember it. Not so. *Nightly News* reported on the civil war in Lebanon for something like seven years, in dozens of pieces, many of which went beyond the shootings and bombings. And when the Lebanese crisis of 1982 erupted with the Israeli invasion, there was a tendency to use the same old shorthand, based on the assumption that people remembered what we had reported before on the situation and the alliances there. We had given them the facts, but we were missing the point. The public needed that information repeated; people had quite understandably forgotten what had been reported before, and they needed an update. But when the Israelis marched in, the stories were so filled with action that there was hardly time for backgrounding. It's a real problem, for everybody in the business.

In writing about government and politics, a lot of stories are word stories. What happened was that somebody said something. And all on television. The 1980 Democratic National Convention wasn't long on drama—except when Senator Edward M. Kennedy came in defeat to address the delegates.

Here's part of the AP story on that convention session:

> NEW YORK (AP)—Sen. Edward M. Kennedy, cheered to the rafters at the Democratic National Convention that crushed his challenge to President Carter, won endorsement of his $12 billion job creation program as part of the campaign platform Tuesday night.
>
> It was one of three Kennedy planks approved in voice votes amid cheers and chants of "We Want Ted."
>
> House Speaker Thomas P. O'Neill Jr. pronounced them passed and a fourth contested plank, which included Kennedy's call for wage and price controls, rejected.
>
> On the latter, he said "the nos were the clear winners," a verdict less evident to listeners without gavels.
>
> It was all part of a deal engineered by telephone to avoid a showdown roll call on the Kennedy planks at a convention that spent nearly 40 minutes in cheering, sign-waving demonstration for the conquered Kennedy.
>
> Carter lieutenants acknowledged that the platform package was negotiated to approval because of the likelihood that the convention would have adopted the jobs plan had the issue been pushed to a roll call vote. But they also said Carter would spell out his differences with the platform on Tuesday.
>
> Kennedy came to Madison Square Garden, Carter's victory arena, to urge the adoption of his economic proposals into the Democratic platform.
>
> He stayed to speak of a campaign waged and lost: "Often we sailed against the wind but always we kept our rudder true. . . ."
>
> It was an hour of high emotion at a businesslike convention, the hall erupting into cheers for the man the dele-

gates would not nominate. Blue and white Kennedy campaign signs waved across the convention floor; for the
moment even the Carter delegates put aside their green
placards to cheer the loser in a gesture of unity.

That gives a sampler of Kennedy's words—there were more,
lower in the story—describes the convention action, and explains the Carter reaction.

Events dictated the construction of the first few paragraphs.
Kennedy had come to the convention in defeat, and it had
endorsed a platform provision favored by his side and opposed
by Carter.

The fourth and fifth paragraphs are there, and prominent,
because they describe the deal that led to the outcome.
Kennedy's rhetoric made for more enjoyable reading, but it had
to wait.

It was more important that the President in victory had to
acquiesce to the platform demands of the loser, and that he
would soon be issuing a dissent from the platform of his own
party.

There was humor in the description of O'Neill's announcement of what the convention had and hadn't decided. He determined the outcome in keeping with the Carter-Kennedy deal;
the relative numbers of shouted yeas and nays sounded like a
vote for the Kennedy planks every time.

There was a touch of analysis in the explanation of the deal,
and there was color in the scene and situation.

The idea was to deliver the facts and hold the interest of
readers who more than likely had seen the whole thing themselves, courtesy of television. All those things are worth doing
whether that's a factor or not. But the kind of communication
that makes new information old in a hurry also makes those
touches vital.

There are traps to beware, particularly in word stories—
stories in which the news is what somebody said. After you've

said "said" a dozen times, you tend to start looking for synonyms, figuring the reader will get as tired of seeing that verb as the writer is tired of using it.

That is a temptation to resist. "Said" is a spare, unobtrusive, utilitarian word. The temptation can produce such words as "conceded," or "acknowledged," or "claimed," or "asserted." Or even "averred," which is stuffy enough for lawyers, but of no utility to newswriters.

All but the last are useful, but they aren't synonyms. Each carries a special meaning. If that is what you mean, use it. But it is easy to slant a story without meaning to, just by switching words in an effort to avoid repetition.

Some stories stand still for you; they've happened, they're over, and you can write them. Breaking stories, which unfold as you write, present a different set of problems.

Some breaking stories, like space shots and inaugurations, are predictable and can almost be written in advance. Some are; occasionally a story will be written before it happens. The President takes office at noon on January 20. That can be written the day before, and ready for print when it happens. Best not to put it into print before it happens. The AP once did with a story about UN Secretary General Dag Hammarskjöld's arrival on an African trip. He died in an airplane crash on the way.

It is the sudden story that presents the greater challenge— the catastrophe, the resignation, the airplane crash. Or the shooting of a President.

At 2:31 P.M. on March 30, 1981, this bulletin moved on the wires of the Associated Press.

> WASHINGTON (AP)—Several gunshots were fired at President Reagan as he left a downtown Washington hotel today.
>
> Secret Service agents shoved the president into his armored limousine, which sped away from the Washington Hilton Hotel, leaving three men lying on the ground only

a few feet from where Reagan had been standing.
Reagan was apparently unharmed.

What was apparent in that first bulletin was not so. He was
harmed. But nobody knew that for the better part of an hour.
As fresh information arrived, the story took shape. Press Secretary James S. Brady had been wounded, as had two security
men. The White House said Reagan hadn't been hit.

Then that changed. Reagan had been wounded.

The wire services had to deliver running stories, constantly
updated with developments, for afternoon newspapers, and for
morning newspapers. Before the day and night were out, the
AP had revised each of its running stories thirteen times.

In wire service work, each of those revisions is called a lead.
The term stems from the fact that each successive lead picks up
in the body of the previous story, preserving the portion of the
prior copy that hasn't changed.

Here's part of the thirteenth lead delivered to morning newspapers:

> WASHINGTON (AP)—President Reagan was shot in the
> chest Monday by a youthful gunman who tried to assassi-
> nate him in a blaze of .22-caliber pistol fire that critically
> injured White House Press Secretary James S. Brady.
>
> Reagan "sailed through surgery" according to doctors
> who said he'd be ready to make presidential decisions by
> Tuesday.
>
> But Brady was said to be fighting for his life, a bullet
> through his brain.
>
> Dr. Dennis O'Leary said "a really mangled bullet" was
> removed from Reagan's left lung. He said the president's
> condition was stable, the prognosis excellent, and that the
> president would probably be hospitalized for about two
> weeks.
>
> "Honey, I forgot to duck," Reagan told his wife as he
> was wheeled into surgery. Then he told the doctors he
> hoped they were Republicans.

A Secret Service agent and a policeman also were wounded in the mid-afternoon incident outside a Washington hotel where Reagan had just addressed a union convention. They were reported in serious condition, but apparently not in danger.

A youthful, sandy-haired gunman from suburban Denver was wrestled into handcuffs and arrested moments after the assailant leveled his pistol at the president and fired six times from near point-blank range. The Secret Service identified him as John Warnock Hinckley, 25, of Evergreen, Colo.

There was no known motive, no explanation for the savage burst of gunfire that exploded as the president stood beside his limousine, ready to step inside for the one-mile ride back to the White House.

The vital fact dictated the lead. A President had been shot and wounded. That had to come first.

After that, every paragraph had to reflect a decision.

Brady's name was in the lead because his was the life in danger. (There were reports that day that his life had been lost. They were broadcast on television, and the AP reported that Senate Majority Leader Howard H. Baker, Jr., had been told Brady was dead. Those stories were wrong.)

The second paragraph says in a sentence that Reagan underwent successful surgery.

The third describes Brady's condition and wounds.

Then back to Reagan for a paragraph that tells where he was wounded—the left lung—and gives the doctor's report on his condition and prospects.

Reagan's quips became important for what they told the nation about his condition and his spirit. That's why two of them are high in this story.

It was essential to report quickly the injury of the other two men, and to describe their condition. Hence the next paragraph, which might better have been closer to the lead.

The lead already had told of the gunman; the seventh paragraph gives detail and a name.

The eighth tells of the mystery that surrounded his motives that first night, describes the scene of the shooting, and gives the geography—one mile from the White House.

That's not to say that the story couldn't have been told better, or that the sequence had to be that sequence. But it does flow with some order, and it does so because each element was assigned its place for a reason.

Some people outline stories before they write. In handling a story like the Reagan shooting, there isn't time.

To write under that kind of pressure, you need to put together an outline in your mind. That takes practice. The only way to learn it is to do it.

For openers, practice at stories that describe unfolding events. They can be handled with narrative, the lead on top, the rest of the story unfolding on paper much as it unfolded to the writer. Sometimes the simplest construction is the most effective.

Take the day American astronauts landed on the moon.

The most compelling story words could tell—to people who already had seen incredible pictures on their television sets— was just this:

Man walked on the moon today, Sunday, July 20, 1969.

For all of that, there are no easy guidelines to get a writer from the lead through all the choices that determine what belongs in the story, what doesn't, and what goes where.

The best rule is that what interests a writer who knows his subject is most likely to interest the reader.

There is a technique that comes with time and practice. It helps shape the story and make it flow. It also makes the copy difficult to cut, and so annoys meddlesome editors, which is a fringe benefit, and fun.

That is to make one paragraph flow into the next. Look for

transitional words and lines. When they fit, use "so," or "and," or "but," or "besides" at the start of sentences. Don't overdo it, but it will work now and then.

Done properly, it ties the story together. That makes it more likely that the sequence is logical, that the facts and ideas do flow one from another. It also makes the writing more enjoyable, which is almost certain to do the same for the reading of it.

Here is a story on the presidential nomination of Gerald R. Ford at the 1976 Republican National Convention, written so that almost every paragraph meshes with the next.

KANSAS CITY, MO. (AP)—Gerald R. Ford, a plainspoken man who gained the White House in extraordinary times, won the Republican presidential nomination early Thursday in the tumult of a divided national convention.

Then, two hours after midnight, he stood at the side of his vanquished challenger and told Ronald Reagan: "I congratulate you for a fine campaign . . ."

By a 117-vote margin, Ford defeated at last the fierce conservative challenge waged by Reagan, the unrelenting rival whose candidacy kept the prize in doubt until the eve of Republican decision.

They parted with a warm handshake, after vowing unity and professing mutual admiration in a brief, nationally televised news conference.

The Republican National Convention's first ballot gave Ford 1,187 votes, 57 more than the majority he needed. Reagan received 1,070.

While some Reagan delegates wept in the bitterness of their defeat, Ford rejoiced briefly with his staff, then left his hotel for a 25-block trip that symbolized the urgency of his quest for unity.

For presidents customarily are called upon, and this time, Ford was the caller.

He conferred with Reagan in the challenger's suite at the Alameda Plaza Hotel. Ford said they discussed the vice presidential selection the president would announce about 12 hours later.

A story written with transitions, one paragraph to the next, is a story more likely to hold the interest of a reader than a piece that is not woven together.

Besides, when that editor shows up with his blue pencil and tries to lop out elements you thought important, he'll have a hell of a time with sentences and paragraphs that are tied together. It's much easier to edit paragraphs away when there aren't any links to the paragraphs that precede and follow.

And one of the facts of newswriting life is that there'll always be an editor out there, determined to take out something you've labored to put into the story.

His job is to edit, and he probably won't be deterred. But if you've done your writing job, he'll have to think hard about what to take out. At least as hard as you thought about what to put in.

And all of that work will make it a better story.

4 *COLOR*

R EAL things happen to real people in real places, people who bleed and sweat in Victorian hospitals or run-down courthouses, who wear double knits or tweeds, Rolexes or Timexes, and who, under stress, say wonderful or terrible things.

It is said that genius lies in the details. Good newswriting also lies in the details. It is the job of the writer to weave these threads of life into the story, to add authenticity and character to the bones of fact and circumstance.

That is called color, and it has a place in every kind of newswriting, from editorials to obituaries.

News is not fiction, but it can be exciting. People who make news usually have something interesting in their character. The reason stories get in the paper or on the air is that they describe out-of-the-ordinary events, or people, or both.

It's up to the writer to point up the extraordinary elements that take a story out of the so-what category.

Color comes in all shapes and forms. It is sometimes a small fact, such as what someone ate or wore. It is sometimes the writer's own observation of the weather, or the landscape, or the look on the face of the accused when the sentence is passed. It can be, and often is, a single word.

It can be just about anything that adds life and flavor to what are sometimes derisively called "the bare facts."

Bare fact: Two teenagers die in a car crash. Color: One was wearing a T-shirt with the inscription "I'm not here for a long time, I'm here for a good time."

Bare fact: A President makes a lengthy and eloquent speech without notes. Color: He practiced all day.

Bare fact: Millions watch a television series about a Japanese warlord. Color: Sales of Japanese sake in liquor stores rise dramatically.

Bare fact: The price of ham goes down. Color: The price of eggs does not.

There are two broad categories of color: descriptive and reportorial. The writer who thinks to check on the price of eggs, or the sales of sake, is making his story richer and better through reporting.

Descriptive color requires observation. Gulls wheeling in the air over the shipwreck. The sun coming out when the wedding ends. Homer's "wine-dark sea."

(Homer had a way with a phrase. As far as we know, he was the first to write "smiling through her tears," although some rewrite man may have put that in.)

Good descriptive color does not require a lot of fancy language. Here is John McPhee, writing about a destroyed neighborhood in Atlantic City he visited one night:

> The sidewalks of St. Charles Place have been cracked to shards by through-growing weeds. There are no buildings. Mansions, hotels once stood here. A few street lamps now drop cones of light on broken glass and vacant space behind a chain-link fence that some great machine has in places bent to the ground. Five plane trees—in full summer leaf, flecking the light—are all that live on St. Charles Place.

McPhee does not call the place abandoned or burned out or devastated. The devastation is described in spare, simple lan-

guage which leaves the reader with a full picture of what was
to be seen that night. And had McPhee written that for television, as narrative copy with pictures, it would have been just as
effective. Good color does not have to resort to rhetoric. If a
scene is sufficiently moving to merit a paragraph, it will offer
its own inventory of facts to be recorded.

McPhee's St. Charles Place took a full paragraph, but most
news stories don't have room for color at that length. Descriptive color usually must be compressed into a word or two, or
at most a phrase. That brings writers perilously close to steam-
ing jungles, left-leaning regimes, oil-rich sheikhdoms in the
troubled Middle East, and old man winter. There is a wire
service legend about a weather story that began: "Old Man
Winter shoved an icy finger into Dixie today." Some color.

Clichés are quick phrases which once were fresh and shining,
but have lost their utility. A cliché is a white dwarf of the
language, hanging on to existence but of no value.

Avoid hyphenated gimmicks such as crisis-prone, debt-ridden, death-defying, tortoise-paced and emotion-charged. These
cover a lot of ground very briefly, but their use makes the
writing hackneyed. And keep in mind that people don't say
things like "I saw debt-ridden Charles Smith at the bank
today." Nor do they speak of "embattled" mayors or "belea-
guered" secretaries of state. Newswriters sometimes do; real
people don't.

That is not color, only a bad habit. It also is a common one.
Some phrases of that ilk are so ingrained as to be virtually
automatic: security is always tight, the South Bronx is always
blighted, the Middle East is always troubled. A problem is no
greater a problem when it is described as thorny. Death can be
expected or unexpected, fast or slow, painful or serene, but it
does not help the sentence to call it tragic. In fact, most deaths
are not tragic. Few people die because of a flaw in character,
which is the essential element of tragedy. They just die.

Newswriting will always call for quick, bright characterizations of people and descriptions of events. *Time* magazine set a pattern for this kind of writing in the 1920s when its editors decided that most people mentioned in *Time* needed two words of description before their name. One of the words usually referred to physical characteristics, the other to character values.

Thus T. S. Eliot, the poet, was described as bespectacled, shy T. S. Eliot. Johnny Mercer, the songwriter, took note of this in a song he wrote called "Balding, affable me." *Time* abandoned the style in the 1940s, along with a rule, unwritten but enforced, that whenever Mayor Fiorello La Guardia of New York was mentioned, he had to be described as shaped like a fireplug.

Some people, however, *are* shaped like fireplugs and can be so described, when it helps to make the story more understandable. But only then, not with a rule that requires a put-down. La Guardia also was a combative and outspoken mayor who read the funny papers on the radio during a newspaper strike. That does a lot more to bring him alive to a reader now than does a description of his physique. Television is one reason: It has changed the rules. In the TV age, people are accustomed to seeing their political leaders. It doesn't help the story to write about public figures as though the reader had never seen them. If a man everyone has seen on television has no hair, you don't accomplish anything by writing that he's bald. It takes a closer look than that. If he's been in the sun without a hat, and the pate is beet red, use it.

It is sometimes necessary to use a political or ideological description of a politician. Conservative Democrats in the Congress are a well-defined group, and calling them conservatives is part of the story. The same applies to liberals. The middle of the road is harder to define, and also is very crowded. Most politicians, left or right, claim to be moderates. The *Almanac of American Politics* provides charts on all governors, senators and members of the House, showing their ratings by conservative and liberal organizations which judge them by their voting records. When in doubt, leave the description out.

Efforts at labeling can be risky. There's no question Ronald Reagan is a conservative and proud of it. But there are many other people in public life who can't be classified. One way around that is to describe their records in specific terms. He who votes against foreign aid may vote for civil rights bills.

Short labels for people and places can be misleading. It is accurate to describe Pittsburgh as a manufacturing center, or West Side Manhattan Democrats as liberal. But it is far riskier to write of the inhabitants of a Christian village in Lebanon as right-wing.

Walter Laqueur, the political scientist, who used to be a newspaperman himself, writes: "It is perfectly nonsensical to call the inhabitants of a poor Lebanese mountain village 'right wing' because they are Christian, and their neighbors from the next village 'leftist'—just because they are Muslim."

Laqueur also points out the indiscriminate use of the term "guerrilla." He wrote in the *Washington Quarterly,*

> The London *Times* would never report about a major bomb outrage or assassination or kidnapping by "Irish guerrillas" in London, just as *Le Monde* would never refer to Corsican guerrilla fighters in Paris, or *The New York Times* would never use the term guerrillas when reporting the activities of some Puerto Rican extremists in New York. But the same newspapers will not hesitate to report about guerrillas—though they quite obviously mean terrorists—if these happen to operate in other countries. There is a very considerable substantive, not just a semantic, difference between terrorist and guerrilla; furthermore, guerrilla has, on the whole, a positive public relations image, which terrorist has not.

"Guerrilla" is a Spanish word, meaning "little war" and referring also to an irregular soldier who fights in small actions. "Terrorist" comes from the "reign of terror" in the French Revolution. "Guerrilla" is an accurate word to use in military situations, as in attacks on troops. "Terrorist" is appropriate when used to describe those who attack civilians for political reasons. The distinction is important. Politicians almost never bother to make it, and it is quotes from the politicians that can give you trouble—even when you know the difference.

Just keep in mind that one side's terrorist is the other side's freedom fighter.

It is tempting, sometimes, to use superlatives as color. The longest meeting, the greatest number of complaints, the tallest flagpole. These are sometimes called "Guinnessisms," after the *Guinness Book of World Records,* a handy volume to have nearby.

But beware. Don't stretch for superlatives. If the Israeli Air Force has been flying ten sorties a day regularly, it is accurate to say that eleven sorties is a record number of air strikes, but it is misleading. Some writers reach for firsts, or mosts, and end up writing that this or that happened for the first time on a rainy Thursday. That's journalistic junk food.

It's often wrong, and frequently funny. Charles Schulz made fun of the practice in one of his *Peanuts* comic strips. Snoopy leads his troop of Cub Scout birds to the top of a hill and announces, "Do you realize that we are about to set a record? We are the first hikers ever to climb this peak and then sit here eating angel food cake with seven-minute frosting!" One of the birds offers Snoopy an autograph.

Nothing has to be the first, or the most, or the biggest, to be colorful, or to be news. Superlatives should be approached with extreme caution. As soon as you write that something happened for the first time, a dozen people will advise you that it happened before. Unless your reporting proves the superlative, hedge the bet. Make it one of the first, or among the biggest.

When in doubt, proceed on the assumption that everything has happened before.

Be equally careful with absolutes. If something is supposed to be final, unique, absolute, or whatever, make sure it is so.

Then make sure again. Those words mean what they say.

Many a good news story has been ruined by a reporter who wasn't satisfied that what had happened was unusual, and overwrote to make it unprecedented.

Color is best produced with details, not with adjectives. If the mural is painted in bright greens and reds, write that instead of "brightly colored." If the house is luxurious, try to estimate its price. If the fur coat dazzles, say if it's mink or sable. A fat man is a fat man, but a 285-pound man is better. Work at it.

Detail is the heart of color. When Henry Luce started *Time* magazine, he searched for a way to make its stories appear more authentic than the competition's. He began what might be called the what-did-the-President-have-for-breakfast school of newswriting. Luce was after authenticity, and he sought it in the lives of the newsmakers. Food, wardrobe, private habits, favorite colors or books—all ended up in the magazine, adding what he believed was verisimilitude to the reporting. What Mr. Roosevelt ate in the morning didn't have anything to do with what he did during the day, but many a *Time* reporter had to stand up at press briefings on serious matters to ask what the President had for breakfast.

Relevance is the key to skillful use of adjectives and adverbs. The modifiers must help define the noun or the verb.

Here, too, details can do it. If a speech is an hour and ten minutes long, write that. Or better, write seventy minutes. Don't call it lengthy. It will take time to find the specific, but it is worth doing. If something happened several years ago, find out when it happened. Use the date. Touches like that tell a reader that you know what you're talking about.

Luce was right. Color does add authenticity. It may not be essential to know that when medals were handed out for valor, some of the wounded recipients had to be helped to the platform. But it makes the story. A fact like that can be added in a phrase, a sentence, or a few words in the lead. It's best if not too much is made of it. Color that dominates the story is superimposed. Descriptive detail that flows as part of the story adds to the writing, to the reading, and to the information.

Color does not necessarily mean colorful words. It is stilted to write: "A courageous fireman risked death last night when he drove a truck into the blazing holocaust of an oil refinery fire to save the lives of 16 workers trapped in a sea of burning gasoline."

Better to write: "Sixteen workers trapped in a burning oil refinery were rescued last night by a lone fireman who drove a truck across a sea of flaming gasoline to bring them to safety."

"Lone fireman" points up the heroism of the fireman, an important element in the story. "Sea of burning gasoline" is a vivid way to describe the nighttime scene. But it is not necessary to pin the label "courageous" on the fireman, or to add "blazing holocaust" to the sea of burning gasoline.

"Less is more" has been used as advice to architects. It's a good rule for all writers. If you've got a good yarn, you can drop in the color sparingly, only where it helps. If you don't have a good story, all the color in the world won't dress it up.

Color and adjectives are not synonyms. Too many adjectives can choke the color, if not the life, out of a story.

Here are two AP leads written on the assassination of Robert F. Kennedy, the first from Los Angeles, where he died, the second from New York, where his body was taken.

> LOS ANGELES—Robert F. Kennedy, felled like his president brother by an assassin's bullet, died early today.
>
> His mourning family prepared to take his body home to New York, across the nation Kennedy had hoped to lead as president.
>
> Kennedy, 42, never regained consciousness, never showed signs of recovery, after a savage burst of revolver fire sent a bullet plunging into his brain—at the pinnacle of his own campaign for the White House.

There are a couple of adjectives that pass for color in that copy. Obviously the family mourned, and bursts of revolver fire aimed at people are by definition savage.

But when Kennedy's body was flown back to Manhattan, the adjectives really burst forth, and got in the way of the story.

That produced copy so full of manufactured color that it omitted the central fact of the story: Robert Kennedy was dead.

> NEW YORK—Robert F. Kennedy came home across the full majestic breadth of springtime America Thursday to New York, his adopted state, where he found political haven in the doleful aftermath of his brother's assassination.

That's six adjectives in a sentence that tells of John Kennedy's assassination—but never mentions the assassination of Robert Kennedy.

To paraphrase the cigarette warning: Caution. Adjectives can be hazardous to your story.

There is color everywhere—in the sky, in trees and plants, in buildings, in the way people dress and talk.

One of the best writers ever to work for news magazines used to carry a book on plants when he went on assignment. Dwight Martin found that his copy was given extra polish when he was able, accurately, to describe the local landscape. In Southeast Asia, he wrote of the sound of the bullets in the tamarind trees.

If you don't know what kind of trees stand next to the courthouse, ask. Too many reporters are embarrassed to ask questions like that.

Knowledge of buildings and architectural styles is useful. It is one thing to write that the kidnapping took place in a tree-shaded mansion on the outskirts of town. It is quite another thing to report that it happened in a colonnaded antebellum mansion on a day when the honeysuckle was in bloom—but not all in the same sentence, please.

When weather is part of a story, a thermometer can make a

difference. On a campaign swing in the summer, everyone will know that the candidate is perspiring. Not everyone, however, will be able to write that the temperature was 93 degrees in the shade. You don't have to be at the North Pole or in the Sahara to make copy out of the weather.

During the cold war, in the 1950s, few American news organizations had correspondents in Moscow, and the reporting from the Soviet Union was heavily censored. *Time* magazine would often cable the Associated Press in Moscow, asking what the weather was like on a particular day. It was the only color the magazine could get.

There's a place, and a need, for color in all kinds of newswriting, print or broadcast. But techniques differ between the two, and within broadcast journalism itself.

Radio and television require different approaches. Radio is a good medium for the transmission of abstractions, of ideas. You can read poetry on radio, but it is not as easy to read poetry effectively into a television camera. The same is true of history, of personalities, even of philosophy.

Radio coverage of a state funeral, for example, can make the best use of quotations from the deceased. When Sir Winston Churchill was buried, the procession took hours, and all of those hours could have been filled with quotations from his books and speeches.

Television is something else. And there are differences within television. A Canadian communications scholar, some years ago, set up two test groups of college students on the day of a state funeral in Ottawa. One group watched on black-and-white television. The other watched on a color set. The reporting was identical on both sets.

But when the students wrote essays on what they saw, the ones who watched in black-and-white described the number of people in the church, the length of the funeral cortege, what was said in the eulogies—all specifics. The students who watched in color, however, wrote about duty and country and patriotism, and paid little attention to the specifics.

The conclusion, obviously, is that events observed on color television bring out different feelings than events observed in black-and-white. No one seems to know why.

It helps to remember that people in a radio audience are concentrating on the words, while on television the audience must cope with both words and pictures. That is why writing color for radio, especially a radio documentary, is the simplest of all broadcast writing. It can also be the best. Someone schooled in, and skilled at, writing for print will have little difficulty writing narration for a radio documentary.

Writing for someone who is to read a radio newscast calls for a slightly different approach. Unless it is handled carefully, color can sound like the opinion of the newscaster. Overdone color sounds staged and theatrical. Don't ham it up.

Jet engines wail, explosions sound thunderous, hand grenades go off with a sharp, nasty little crack. Victims scream and dogs bay at the moon. But a newscast on radio is a brief summary of facts, and descriptions of that kind don't belong in the newscaster's copy. The newscaster must be factual and neutral. Best to say the sound of the explosion was heard five miles away, because that is part of the story. But unless people mistook the sound for thunder, and said so, there's no need to try to increase the drama with the word "thunderous." Something heard five miles away is a big bang. Equal care must be given to quotations, so that listeners don't think the newscaster is saying it himself. Quotations should not only be introduced, but in radio, they often have to be ended so the listener knows the quotation is over. This is not as important on a short, simple quote as it is on one that runs two or three sentences. When a quotation is lengthy, the audience too often thinks it's the newscaster speaking for himself, and not the news source. It's easy for a listener to forget that something was said by a relative of a victim. The quote should be closed by a phrase such as: "Those words from the victim's father."

While announcers reading written copy should be sparing in the use of color, reporters at the scene have much greater flexibility. Radio is swift and immediate. It takes the listener where he cannot go. Whether radio reporters are at the summit conference in Geneva or the wreck on the interstate, they must always remember that they are somewhere the listeners aren't. "Here" is one of the most valuable words in the radio reporter's vocabulary. Here in Geneva tonight . . . Here on the interstate, where the cars are jammed up as far as I can see . . . Radio reporters shouldn't be afraid of the first person, especially when writing color. If the reporter felt the heat of the burning building from across the street, the reporter should say so. Radio reporters don't work for the New York *Times*. They are often shock troops, first on the scene, and their reports should be vivid, immediate, and filled with description.

The man who set the style for much radio reporting was Edward R. Murrow of CBS. His reporting from London during the German bombing of 1940 is an example of the basic principles of the craft. Here is Murrow, on a London rooftop during an air raid:

> I think probably in a minute we shall have the sound of the guns in the immediate vicinity. The lights are swinging over in this general direction now. There they are! That was the explosion overhead, not the guns themselves. I should think in a few minutes there may be a bit of shrapnel around here. Coming in, moving closer all the while.
>
> The plane's still very high. Earlier this evening we could hear occasional—again, those were explosions overhead. Earlier this evening we heard a number of bombs go sliding and slithering across, to fall several blocks away. Just overhead now the burst of the antiaircraft fire. Still the nearby guns are not working. The searchlights now are feeling almost directly overhead. Now you'll hear two bursts a little nearer in a moment.
>
> There they are! That hard stony sound.

Murrow spoke directly to the listeners: "We shall have the sound of the guns . . ." He used the first person: "I should think . . ." He explained what was going on: "Now you'll hear . . ." He described the noises: "There they are!"

That was a big story. The principles are the same today for radio reporters on stories big or small. Television is usually regarded as a more glamorous place to work, but for immediacy, and the quick responses required, radio can't be beaten.

Murrow was also a fine writer. In one of his wartime commentaries, he described the scene in a Mayfair hotel, where he saw "many old dowagers and retired colonels settling back on the overstuffed settees in the lobby. It wasn't the sort of protection I'd seek from a direct hit from a half-ton bomb, but if you were a retired colonel and his lady you might feel that the risk was worth it because you would at least be bombed with the right sort of people."

That was written copy, not ad-libbed, and it is an example of another principle of radio reporting. Write it the way you would say it. Read the copy aloud to see if it sounds conversational. If something makes you laugh or cry, share it with the audience. Think of an audience as one intelligent friend. Tell that friend what you've found out.

The television newscaster, the person in the studio, follows a different set of rules. The newscaster has to maintain the neutral detachment of the radio newsreader, but on television the audience gets to watch a real person reading the news: a person with a face, mannerisms, smiles and frowns.

The television newscaster must transmit color without endorsing it, or making it part of the newscaster's own personality. (Some don't believe this, and try to make themselves as dramatic as the news they're reporting. The term in the trade for these people is "hot dogs," and this book is not written for them.)

The easiest way to handle color in a television newscast is to put it in someone else's mouth. Use a quote, and make sure the audience knows it's a quote. Don't say the fire at the orphanage was ghastly; see if a witness said it.

Stick to the facts. If the philanthropist arrived in his Rolls-Royce, say so. The goal is to make the copy sound conversational. You would not say to a friend, "Silver-haired Barry Goldwater made a speech today." Don't say it on television. You might say of Goldwater, conversationally, "still going strong, after a quarter of a century in the Senate." That can be worked into television copy.

Don't say on your own that Barry Goldwater is the conscience of the conservatives. That's a mantle some others would claim for themselves. Besides, you don't have to say it on your own—he said it. The title of Goldwater's first book was *Conscience of a Conservative*.

Television newscasters are individuals, and they handle color in individual ways. The thing to remember is that the newscaster's relationship to the audience is a personal one. It is impossible to think of thousands or millions in an audience; the wise newscaster thinks of one or two people watching, and handles his color conversationally.

The same rule applies to the spoken word on television in situations where most of the copy has to be ad-libbed—at parades, county fairs, funerals, political conventions, inaugurations, space shots, festivals, elections, any special event. But in these situations, the conversational tone has to be carefully disciplined.

The narrator for television special events has to remember that a picture is, in fact, worth a thousand words. The good narrators learn to shut up when the picture is strong. And when they do talk, they are careful not to describe what the audience is already watching, but to find something to say which supplements that image.

When the motorcade enters the stadium, the audience can see it on their screens. There is no need to say the motorcade is entering the stadium, but that is the most common mistake made by television journalists. Better to talk about how many people are in the stadium, or how long it took the motorcade to get there, or talk about the weather, than to describe what the audience can see.

Those who have done their homework may be able to say something funny or interesting about the stadium itself, for they have uncovered the most valuable secret of ad-libbing on television: "homework," and it is more important than anything else.

Most events run late. A broadcaster must be prepared to talk for long periods of time without advance notice. Those who haven't done their homework blather. Those who know their subject can talk for hours, without being repetitive.

One of the most successful reporters of special events for television was the late Richard Dimbleby, of the British Broadcasting Corporation. He was a gifted broadcaster, writer and reporter, and he did more homework than any of his contemporaries. On one occasion, he was on the air at the Royal Needlework School in London, where the queen mother was to make an appearance. Dimbleby described the items on display, talked about the school's history, and then it came time for the royal appearance. But the queen mother didn't appear, so Dimbleby went around again, talking about needlework in China, Japan, Persia and Europe, describing different stitches and techniques as though he had spent his life with a needle in his hand. When the queen mother appeared, twenty-five minutes later, she explained that she'd been watching all this on television in her palace nearby, and became so interested in what Dimbleby had been saying that she had forgotten the time.

The fact is, Dimbleby knew nothing about needlework twenty-four hours earlier, but he'd done his homework the night before.

Dimbleby's audiences were enormous. When the British Commonwealth hooked up to the BBC, the telecast often was watched by 300 million people. And on occasion, the 300 million listened to Dimbleby fill the time. Princess Margaret was fifty minutes late to her wedding in 1960. Dimbleby, however worried he may have been privately about running out of material, ad-libbed gracefully and informatively.

(Dimbleby's most difficult peacetime assignment may have come on the night when the BBC pushed him out on a roof to report on a fog so thick it had shut London down. He talked for hours, unable to see a thing.)

Richard Dimbleby had a natural talent for this kind of broadcasting, but he brought it to perfection through much study. He knew history, protocol and a good deal about the people he was describing. When a pope traveled to the Holy Land, Dimbleby turned up with a large briefcase jammed with small file cards, arranged by subject, each group wrapped in a rubber band. With them, he could talk for hours about the pope, the places he would visit, and the history of the place.

American broadcasters who cover space come prepared in a similar way. When a hold is called in a launch countdown, there is nothing more satisfying than the knowledge that the research provides more than can possibly be said about the launch.

Preparation. You can't do too much of it. A. J. Liebling of the *New Yorker,* one of the best writers of his time, once wrote of preparation:

> One of the best preps I ever did was for a profile of Eddie Arcaro, the jockey. When I interviewed him, the first question I asked was "How many holes longer do you keep your left stirrup than your right?" Most jockeys on American tracks ride longer on their left side.
>
> That started him talking easily, and after an hour, during which I had put in about twelve words, he said, "I can see you've been around riders a lot."

"I had," wrote Liebling, "but only during the week before I was to meet him."

One final word for broadcasters who may have to talk a lot:

Don't swear in ordinary conversation. Swearing tends to limit your vocabulary, particularly when it comes to adjectives. People who swear a lot often find themselves tongue-tied when they have to clean up their speech. If you're going to do color, spoken or written, you need those adjectives, and often you need them in a hurry.

You also need a sense of humor, and an appreciation of the ironies and vicissitudes of life.

Sometimes it is simply the addition of a word or a phrase to an otherwise routine story. Sometimes it is called looking for an angle. Dog bites man. Big deal. But suppose the man sits on the board of the local ASPCA. An angle!

A lot of what newspeople write and report is episodic and predictable. There are thousands of fires every year, fifty thousand deaths on the highways annually, people shoot each other with numbing regularity, and the world is constantly troubled.

Cats get caught in trees, presidents win or lose elections, the Soviet grain harvest is damaged by the sixty-second consecutive year of unusually bad weather—just about everything has happened before, in one way or another.

What keeps it interesting? Good reporting, good writing, enthusiastic journalists who think that what they do is important and fun.

Colorful writing is a phrase that has itself become a cliché. There's a better way to describe it: thorough reporting. Sometimes it is as easy as looking around. Sometimes it takes an hour in the files, or an extra telephone call. Or two.

Either way, it's worth the effort. Color is part of the pleasure of writing. You have to look for it, work at it, but when it is woven into the story, it can make all the difference.

5 ANALYSIS

Analysis is to the writer of news what perspective is to the painter of pictures. It provides background and context.

Journalism is not a bulletin board of unrelated events. Unless the reader is told of the connections these events have with what has happened before, or what may happen in the future, reporting the news becomes a disjointed recitation of facts.

A fire of mysterious origin destroys a warehouse. How many other suspicious fires have there been recently in warehouses? The answer to that question can supply analysis.

The city council proposes to make some downtown streets one-way. How has that worked in cities of similar size? That is information which broadens the story with analysis.

The President hints that he might propose wage and price controls. The record shows he was against them six months ago. That's part of the story, and it's news analysis.

Spiro T. Agnew tried to give news analysis a bad name. Then he got one himself, and had to resign as Vice-President.

But his gripe lives, for politicians always have been—always will be—galled by the comments of writers who don't agree with them.

74

Agnew's 1969 speech was a protest against what he called "instant analysis and querulous criticism" of the administration after a nationally televised address by President Richard M. Nixon on the war in Vietnam.

"The audience of seventy million Americans gathered to hear the President of the United States was inherited by a small band of network commentators and self-appointed analysts, the majority of whom expressed in one way or another their hostility to what he had to say," Agnew complained.

Nobody likes criticism, and Presidents like it least of all. Some give the impression that criticizing them is like trampling the flag. And any commentary worth doing is going to sound critical even if it simply adds background or underscores history the President would rather forget. Politicians want to tell it their way.

While Agnew's denunciation was particularly vehement, it was not particularly new.

Lyndon Johnson used to rage at commentary opposing his policies. When a Democratic senator critical of Johnson policy in Vietnam put in a pitch for construction of a dam in his home state, Johnson chewed him out for dissenting on the war. The senator said he'd been impressed by the writings of Walter Lippmann, the columnist, who warned of the perils of escalation. Johnson told him to ask Lippmann for the dam.

Jimmy Carter left office convinced that some columnists are liars. "What hurts as a President responsible for a nation is to see the superficialities and inaccuracies of the press," he said. "Few well-known reporters or columnists will print a story they know is a lie. . . . [but if] they hear a scandalous story, or one that's provocative, they don't want to see it made accurate or see it killed."

He gave no examples and no names. It's unlikely that he could. Journalists who want to keep their jobs don't lie in print or on the air.

CHANCELLOR: Agnew's speech produced an interesting
    reaction at NBC News. Years ago, it was the practice
    to put on members of the opposition party at the end
    of a President's televised address, Democrats after
    Eisenhower, Republicans after Kennedy. The theory
    was that if the President got a crack at a prime-time
    audience, his opposition ought to be given a few
    minutes on the air.
        In 1969, when Agnew made his attack on instant
    analysis, we had abandoned that practice, and were
    even thinking about eliminating the brief recaps by our
    own correspondents. But when Agnew went on the
    attack, there was no way that we would give it up, and
    instant analysis, however brief, is on the air today.

When Dwight D. Eisenhower denounced "sensation-seeking
columnists and commentators" at the 1964 Republican convention, vengeful conservatives roared an ovation and waved
clenched fists at the press stands.
    The late Peter Lisagor of the Chicago *Daily News* proposed
a sacrifice to placate them: "Throw them somebody from the
Chicago *Tribune.*"
    From presidents to mayors to chiefs of police, there's nothing
in the news business more aggravating to those in government
authority than the writings of the columnists, news analysts,
and commentators. They're seen as meddlesome second-guess-
ers, who don't have to make decisions but only stand on the
sidelines and criticize.
    That's true.
    But they aren't self-appointed, as Agnew claimed. It takes
time and a track record for a reporter to reach the point at
which an editor is going to let him write what he thinks instead
of what he has seen or learned.
    There are exceptions, since commentary comes in all shapes
and sizes. Ronald Reagan used to be a radio commentator and

a columnist himself, although not one of those to whom an Agnew or an Eisenhower would have objected.

Politicians and their progeny seldom make very good columnists. They tend to reproduce old speeches and harp on old themes.

But there are exceptions, notably William Safire, who came out of the Nixon White House onto the prestigious op ed page of the New York *Times.* He had a head start, since he'd been a reporter, became an author, and wrote with wit and style. He turned out to be a tenacious investigator, which won him the Pulitzer Prize after only two years in the column business.

It was Safire the political speechwriter who, in 1970, wrote Agnew into a frenzy of alliteration. He has confessed in writing to equipping the campaigning Vice-President with such phrases as "pusillanimous pussyfooters," "vicars of vacillation," "nattering nabobs of negativism," and the never-to-be-forgotten "hopeless, hysterical hypochondriacs of history."

James Reston, the dominant columnist of the *Times,* pronounced the latter offering "the worst example of alliteration in American history."

Safire the columnist has proven a more admirable phrase-maker.

He is even good at writing about what he is good at doing —writing columns. "One idea is a column," Safire decrees. "Trying to fit two ideas into one column tells the reader you couldn't decide what to write about that day. However, three ideas is a pattern, a gestalt, a farrago that illuminates the point, as long as the ideas are related. Four ideas and the column falls apart again.

"Nobody knows why. . . ."

Other offerings from the Safire school of columny:

"The only regular reader today is the irritated reader, and the most successful column is one that causes the reader to throw down the paper in a peak of fit."

"The new columnist should not begin with two columns on

a single subject lest he be slotted for life in that category. If you open with the significance of the population explosion in Ulan Bator, follow with a heartwarmer about nuclear reactors in Dayton and quickly shift to a ripsnorter about the gold standard. Versatility is all: every new columnist must be able to thrill the new customers with his expert-tease."

For the heavyweights, columns are business and business is good. They are widely published, often quoted, in demand for speeches that pay handsomely—$5,000 an appearance for the big names. The datelines are a tip-off to the speechmaking tours that bring in those fees. When a Washington columnist starts writing about the public pulse in university towns in Texas and out-of-the-way cities in Iowa, it's a good bet he's been on the lecture circuit. There are other sidelines too. Some sell insider newsletters to businessmen, or stage their own seminars on what's what in Washington.

"Syndicated columnist" is a phrase with an awesome ring to it. Actually, it doesn't mean much. A syndicate can be a high-powered operation with a stable of noted writers and a long list of customers. Or it can be a run-down office with an old mimeograph machine in the corner to run off the column for Friday's paper and get it in the mail by Tuesday, to be run in a dozen papers.

There are more writers surviving than thriving as columnists. For every big name there are dozens of little ones.

It's a tough business.

It also is very difficult work. Delivering informed opinion in six hundred or seven hundred words, on a set schedule, is exceedingly difficult. Some mornings, you'll wake up without anything to say. But you'll have to say it anyhow. The late Ed Lahey of the Chicago *Daily News* is credited with the observation that writing a column is like being married to a nymphomaniac. As soon as you get through, you have to start again.

The most difficult part of the task is to come up with an idea worth exploring—and then do it again. The three-a-week columnist can't be intermittently profound; there has to be something worth writing—and at best, some reporting to go with it—every other day.

There are reporters' columns, and there are columns without reporting. The latter variety tend to sound pretentious, and to tell the reader what to think, or at least what the columnist thinks people should think.

A. J. Liebling put that category of writer at the bottom of his list of worthies:

"There are three kinds of writers of news in our generation," he wrote. "In inverse order of worldly consideration they are:

"1. The reporter, who writes what he sees.

"2. The interpretive reporter, who writes what he sees and what he construes to be its meaning.

"3. The expert, who writes what he construes to be the meaning of what he hasn't seen."

To get the column to all the customers on time, it has to be written several days in advance. The deadline for next Monday may be this Thursday. That sacrifices timeliness unless the columnist has come up with exclusive material, of which there isn't much. There are more imitation exclusives than real ones, columns that tell of lunch with the ambassador, of little-noticed memoranda, or of speeches that would have been very important at the time they were given except nobody paid any attention.

Jack Germond, the political reporter turned columnist, calls these technical exclusives, by which he means stories that haven't been written because they weren't worth writing.

There is intense competition to generate and explore ideas that *are* worth writing. The *Editor & Publisher* syndicate directory for 1981 lists 178 columns of political commentary, 100 of general commentary, 115 on consumer affairs, 88 on education.

CHANCELLOR: I got to be a commentator after being an anchorman for about twelve years, and I think that experience, and that exposure to the audience, helps me in my work. The audience knows who I am, and the years I spent as a reporter and anchorman have given me—I hope—the experience in news which can be turned into commentary. I see commentary as a kind of logical brief: facts marshaled in such a way as to lead to an inescapable conclusion. At least, inescapable to me. It is part reporting and part analysis. It is not, when it's done properly, some guy sitting there on your television set giving out his opinions on why he doesn't like Senator So-and-so because of the color of his eyes.

MEARS: I write analytical pieces three times a week, at least most weeks. There's no room in AP newswriting for your own opinions, not even in copy labeled analysis. I see what I do pretty much as you described it: to supply background, perspective, explanation, motives. I wouldn't write a piece saying the federal budget system stinks. But when President Reagan called it a Mickey Mouse system, I did one explaining how it is supposed to work and why it doesn't. The hard part, for me, is coming up with ideas. I started doing the column because I wanted to keep writing after I became chief of the Washington bureau. That's always a problem for newsmen who become administrators. You handle budgets, run the complaint desk, worry about expense accounts and overtime forms, try to be sympathetic to the problems of about 120 people on the staff—and try to remember that you used to be a reporter. For me, the writing I'm still able to do is like recess. That's why I got into this line of work in the first place.

Analytical stories, and analytical touches in straight news stories, are handle-with-care business. The pressure of an early deadline can trap a writer into judgments that look silly—or are just plain wrong—when all the facts are in, all the votes are counted.

Take the presidential election of 1960.

Here's the way the New York *Herald Tribune* reported it, in a story written on election night:

> Sen. John F. Kennedy was elected the 35th President of the United States yesterday in a great Democratic victory reminiscent of the heyday of Franklin D. Roosevelt.

It looked that way at deadline time. The East was giving Kennedy a hefty lead over Richard M. Nixon. It didn't stay that way. Tuesday night's landslide became too close to call by early Wednesday. The *Herald Trib* had the right winner. But the editor should have put the period after yesterday.

Kennedy's victory finally was nailed down as the ballots were counted the day after the election. the New York *Times* reported the outcome this way:

> Sen. John F. Kennedy of Massachusetts finally won the 1960 presidential election from Vice President Nixon by the astonishing margin of less than two votes per voting precinct.

When in doubt, wait awhile.

The perils of election-night judgments about the margins and the reasons for the outcome have been eased considerably by public opinion polling.

Still, the lesson of 1960 stands. Make certain the story is nailed down tightly before you try to analyze it. There are few things more embarrassing than to write a learned piece telling why something was as it was—only to discover that it really wasn't.

There are ways around the problem, but they aren't very productive.

When Stalin died in 1953, the New York *Times* carried this analysis:

The fact that appeals for "monolithic unity" and "vigilance" have now become the main theme of Soviet domestic propaganda appears to be a clear indication that the present Soviet rulers fear Premier Stalin's death may result in an explosive resolution of the major tensions now repressed in the Soviet Union.

That's hedged, and then hedged again. It's also dull, and hard to figure out. What all those words add up to is that there's a possibility Russia will blow up now that Stalin is dead. Then again, it may not.

There's nothing wrong with hedging the bet and avoiding absolutes in writing news analysis. But the writer ought to be able to deliver something without qualification. Otherwise the reader who analyzes the analysis will discover that there's not much there.

Sometimes it is better not to write at all.

But editors are a demanding lot. When something big happens, they want an analytical piece to accompany the main story, and they want it now.

Here's the kind of make-believe analysis that can result—again, on the death of Stalin:

> LONDON—Announcement of the death of Prime Minister Joseph Stalin brought few tears in London, but it released a fresh flood of speculation about what will happen next in Russia and what the impact will be on the rest of the world.
>
> The news was received here soon after 1 A.M. London time, when most persons in this country, including government officials and foreign diplomats, were fast asleep. They will hear about it and read about it when they turn on their radios and receive their newspapers at breakfast time.

The story goes on, but that's the best of it. What it says is that Stalin is dead and nobody knows what will result. And that people in London sleep nights.

But that yellowed clipping from the *Herald Trib* does tell a story about the way the news business works. It's a pretty good guess that an editor in New York called or cabled his man in London. "Stalin's died," the message would have gone. "We need a sidebar on what Europe thinks about that."

Our man in London has two comebacks. The sensible one is to reply that Europe doesn't think anything about that right now because Europe is asleep. The trouble is that saying no to an assignment buys nothing but trouble at the home office. Trouble and hostility. After all, it's only 7 P.M. in New York.

"What the hell do we keep you in London for if you can't produce a simple sidebar?" an editor would say. "Your last expense account looks like the national debt. You're always taking a diplomat to lunch on us. You ought to be able to get ahold of some of them now and find out what they think about Stalin."

That leads to comeback No. 2: You write a story even if you don't have one.

It says that London is not in mourning for Stalin. That's some surprise. It then says that his death has stirred speculation about the future in Russia and elsewhere.

The trouble is that there's nobody awake to speculate. So you write about how late it is, when people go to bed in London, and how surprised they'll be when they wake up and learn that Stalin is dead.

There's nothing safer than writing a piece that says next to nothing. Besides, the boss is happy, the next expense account won't be kicked back, and you can go to bed too.

It's not always necessary to turn out a separate analysis piece. Sometimes the explanatory touch can be woven into the news story itself, effectively and objectively. That is a delicate task. You can't write a news story that says, "Here's what this means because I say so," and call it objective reporting.

But there are demonstrable facts that lend meaning, add background, explain. Choose them, write them carefully, and the news story is the better for it.

Ronald Reagan appoints the first woman to the Supreme Court. That made good on a campaign promise, and it was done by a President who had been under criticism for the dearth of women appointees in his administration. Both those facts are demonstrable; both add analytical background.

The ideal analytical touch in a news story comes in a phrase or a sentence that goes one step beyond what happened and says what it means. That can't be opinion; it has to be explanation. It can be a number that makes a complicated tax story more meaningful: Democrats and Republicans have rival tax-cutting proposals, but when you look at it closely, the difference for the average family comes out to $6.50 a month. President Carter says he will not ask for the authority to impose wage and price controls; when he was a candidate he said he would, but it shook up Wall Street and he's got to reassure the financial community.

Japan surrenders and World War II is over. So is an empire, or a dream of one. Here's Homer Bigart in the New York *Herald Tribune:*

> ABOARD USS MISSOURI, TOKYO BAY, Sept. 2—Japan, paying for her desperate throw of the dice at Pearl Harbor, passed from the ranks of the major powers at 9:05 A.M. today when Foreign Minister Mamoru Shigemitsu signed the document of unconditional surrender.

It takes experience and confidence to develop that touch. Done right, the phrase of analysis explains the facts. Done poorly, it smothers them.

Campaigning in 1964, Senator Goldwater wanted to accuse President Johnson of appeasement. He couldn't say it that bluntly; there are certain amenities to be observed in a presidential campaign.

So he said: "the familiar voices of the umbrella carriers are still with us." Neville Chamberlain, umbrella, Munich, appeasement. The equation had to be explained, along with the fact that Goldwater made his accusation by indirection. It wouldn't do to leave the impression that Goldwater was fussing about people who try to stay dry in the rain.

A colleague filed a story explaining the reference in a sentence. It didn't make print that way. An editor back home thought to make it more explicit with this overdone explanation:

> Sen. Goldwater presumably referred to Neville Chamberlain, prime minister of Great Britain from 1937 to 1940. In 1938, Mr. Chamberlain signed the Munich accords with Adolf Hitler, acceding to German territorial demands on Czechoslovakia.
> Mr. Chamberlain customarily carried an umbrella.

Editing like that makes business for bartenders.

At its best, the separate analysis, be it a regularly published column or a sidebar to go with the news of the day, is an essay in logic.

What persuading it does is accomplished by the force of that logic, by explanation, history, background. There are precedents for almost everything that happens. Check, and you'll have clues to the likely outcome of today's events.

Build a case on the record of what has gone before. Seek out the opinions of the experts. State a premise, then support it with facts, from the files and the history books, and by reporting the judgment of the experts. A touch of humor doesn't hurt. Russell Baker pronounced a more telling judgment than all the pundits put together when he translated Jimmy Carter's "moral equivalent of war" energy program into its acronym: MEOW.

The essay in logic is going to tell readers more, and persuade more readers, than the piece that proclaims: "Here is what I have concluded. Go and think likewise."

At least that is so for mortal newsmen. There are exceptions for the select few—very few—who can thunder opinions that influence the decisions of leaders and statesmen.

When Walter Lippmann wrote in the New York *Herald Tribune,* or Arthur Krock in the New York *Times,* Washington listened. Sometimes Washington, or that part of it under their criticism, fumed.

Lippmann on the collapse of the 1960 summit conference after the capture of an American U-2 spy plane inside Russia:

> We must remember that when the plane was captured, Mr. Khrushchev opened the door to the president for a diplomatic exit from his quandary. He did not believe, said Mr. Khrushchev, that Mr. Eisenhower was responsible for ordering the flight. . . .
>
> The diplomatic answer would have been to say nothing at the time or at the most to promise an adequate investigation of the whole affair. Instead, Mr. Eisenhower replied that he was responsible, that such flights were necessary, and then he let the world think, even if he did not say so in exact words, that the flights would continue. This locked the door which Mr. Khrushchev had opened.

A subsequent column, same subject:

> The wound has been made by the series of blunders on the gravest matters in the highest quarters. These blunders have not only angered the Russians and wrecked the summit conference but, much worse than all that, they have cast doubt among our allies and among our own people on our competence to lead the Western alliance on the issues of peace and war.

Lippmann acknowledged that Khrushchev had used harsh and intemperate language in Paris, but his analysis challenged the popular idea that Khrushchev had wrecked the summit.

He wasn't alone in doing so. Here's R. H. Shackford's tough, analytical story from Paris, published in the *Rocky Mountain News* of Denver:

> With a colossal assist by American bungling, Nikita Khrushchev has used the U-2 spy plane episode to provoke an international crisis that will take years to resolve.

Every news analyst makes some wrong judgments and bad calls, but the good ones have a quality essential to good column-writing: the courage to add up the facts and follow their lead, even when that path is unpopular.

Lippmann's reasoning against the U.S. intervention in Vietnam certainly was not popular with Lyndon B. Johnson, then President of the United States. Lippmann wrote in 1965:

> We have never had, at least as far as I know, any straightforward explanation of why the Administration persists in keeping its war aims uncertain. The crucial uncertainty is whether or not the administration intends to impose as yet undefined conditions which must be met before it will agree to a cease-fire or the beginning of negotiations for an armistice.
>
> This uncertainty has seemed to many who are much concerned a deliberate tactic, designed to make the Hanoi government sue for peace before it learns the terms of the peace.

It was a theme Lippmann stressed day after day, in column after column.

In 1966, from Krock, on the expanding war:

> The violence and anti-American direction of the riots against the Ky military junta government in Vietnam support the official finding that Communists are exploiting the popular unrest to further their design to dominate Southeast Asia. But that is merely the latest exercise of a settled policy. And it does not remove the fact that what is occurring is the ripening of the seeds of civil war that tend to be nourished by the military intervention of a totally alien foreign power, however benevolent and high-minded its purpose.

The alien power was the United States, whose government Krock had been covering for more than thirty years.

Because of who they were, what they had done and where they had been, men like Krock and Lippmann could write commentary and render judgments with an impact unrivaled then and unmatched now.

There's something else columnists can do: They can bring to

print stories and subjects that otherwise wouldn't get into the paper. In 1934, Krock wrote of a Washington event that passed almost unnoticed:

> Never was so well publicized a man so neglected by the Washington newspaper corps as was John Maynard Keynes, who spent five or six days here last week. If a report in usually well-informed circles is accurate, that was poor judgment on the part of the correspondents. The British economist is credited with having persuaded the president to step up greatly what is called "inflationary spending."

Keynes would not have been neglected in latter-day Washington. He would have traveled in a maze of microphones and cameras, to and from the network interview programs, every word recorded, written—and analyzed. According to the conservatives, it's people who listened to him who got us into all this economic trouble. Arthur Krock knew a story when he saw one.

There are columnists who can make their judgments stick, or sting, through the force of their prose.

George Will, for example, and Mary McGrory. They write so well that they have to be read.

Here's Will, in full, scholarly bloom, on the 1976 campaign:

> The Thirty Years War began and ended at Prague, the English Civil War at Powick Bridge, World War I at Mons. The presidential campaign is ending where it began, in the Slough of Despond. Many people, including many who will vote for him, feel about Jimmy Carter the way a Roman patrician is said to have felt when he first heard Brutus speak: "I know not what this young man intends, but whatever he intends, he intends vehemently."

Where else could you find out where all those wars ended and, for a bonus, learn what kind of first impression Brutus made?

In the midst of Watergate, Mary McGrory wrote a column about Richard Nixon—and situation comedy:

The town needed a laugh, heaven knows, but who would have thought the president, of all people, would provide us with 45 minutes of low comedy in, of all things, his State of the Union message?

Basically, it was situation comedy. Here was a president facing impeachment, waiting for the multiple indictments of his closest aides, fighting off a court summons from one of the "two finest public servants" he has ever known, hanging onto his great office by his fingernails.

The heavily made-up man on the podium spoke of himself as a miracle worker. . . . The only possible reason for turning him out of office, as he told it, would be that he is too good for us.

That kind of writing is in the style of H. L. Mencken, who offered as good an explanation as any of why columnists can be so aggravating to people who do not agree with them.

"The plain fact is that I am not a fair man and don't want to hear both sides," Mencken once said. "On all subjects, from aviation to xylophone playing, I have fixed and invariable ideas."

His ideas about Calvin Coolidge were fixed and not flattering. "There has been no more trivial and trashy president in American History, nor one surrounded by worse frauds," Mencken wrote.

And of the search for American Communists in an earlier era:

Obviously, the chase of Reds is still a profitable sport in the United States, despite the great scarcity of the game. One seldom picks up a small-town paper without discovering that some retired cavalry captain, or Ku Klux organizer, or itinerant chautauquan has just been in town, alarming the local Babbitts with tales of a Muscovite plot to seize Washington, burn the Capitol, and heave poor Cal into the Potomac.

But for the rest of us, the task is to do the research and the reporting, then construct the case. For most, it is useless and presumptuous to try to influence opinion, but very useful to try to explain what happened and what is likely to follow.

There are many ways to do it.

One is to take an issue that is abstract to most readers, and describe it in real terms. As in:

> KELLY, IOWA (AP)—In the gnawing cold outside Dan Froning's grain warehouse, there is nothing abstract about the issues raised by President's Carter's embargo of shipments to the Soviet Union.
>
> They are as real as the snow-dusted mounds of corn heaped on the pavement because the grain elevator is full; as real as the 30 railroad cars waiting to be loaded with corn that may go nowhere.

That is a lot more effective than writing that Iowa farmers and grain dealers are up in arms over the halt in grain sales ordered by a President who, coincidentally, wanted their votes for renomination.

Another technique is to take what might be written as a straight news story, use the freedom available in analytical copy, and reach judgments about the facts.

John B. Anderson, the former congressman who became an independent presidential candidate in 1980, said over dinner one night in 1978 that he was getting tired of the House and might run for President.

That could have been written without comment or analysis: "WASHINGTON—Rep. John B. Anderson says he is thinking about running for the Republican presidential nomination."

Instead, it was done this way:

> WASHINGTON—To Rep. John B. Anderson, the 1980 Republican presidential campaign is tempting—and temptation now usually means candidacy for the White House later.
>
> "I'm obviously thinking about it," said Anderson.

That was hardly a daring judgment, but it was a judgment and it had to be labeled so. It also was a sound one, not because of any great insight by the writer, but because he'd seen enough politicians in action to know that when one of them says he is thinking about running, he almost always runs.

It was a Ring Lardner character who said, "You could look it up." The rule is a good one. Look up the record and there often will be a story, waiting to be written, that uses yesterday to cast some light on tomorrow.

When President Reagan chose George Bush as his vice-presidential nominee, the more ardent conservatives were outraged. After all, Bush had run against Reagan for the presidential nomination. He who runs against Ronald Reagan must be something other than a conservative, they figured. The record book said otherwise; Bush was a Texas Republican with almost solidly conservative credentials throughout his public career.

The story began:

> DETROIT—Conservative qualms notwithstanding, George Bush is no flaming Republican liberal. He might be a smouldering moderate, and that's enough to make him suspect with some in a GOP world that has turned toward the right.

Analysis can be as simple as putting an event into context. In the 1980 election, the country turned toward the right. An analytical piece put that into perspective:

> WASHINGTON—For years, Republicans have claimed that a great, silent, conservative majority was out there, waiting to arise.
>
> Ronald Reagan got his start in national politics trying to tap that vein in the cause of Barry Goldwater's presidential ticket. That put him on the losing side of a landslide five elections ago.
>
> But the silent majority spoke Tuesday. Led by Presi-

dent-elect Reagan, the conservatives are coming to Washington next year.

It took no genius to see that or write it. The piece put an event into context. Conservative dragon's teeth did not spring into an electoral army overnight. They'd been at work for years, envisioning a Reagan long before there was one available to lead their cause.

Analysis can guide a reader through the thicket of facts that make up any day's news. And the habits that produce it can make any reporter a better reporter.

MEARS: I got a cram course in analytical reporting from Jack Bell, who wrote politics for the AP for years. I was covering Eugene McCarthy's presidential campaign the night President Johnson stunned everybody by saying he wouldn't run again. McCarthy was making a speech at a college outside Milwaukee. Johnson's speech was on television at the same time. At the end of it, he said he wouldn't be a candidate. Gene was in the middle of his speech. I went down to the stage and tried to get his attention, but he kept going. So I went up and interrupted him to tell him LBJ had just quit the campaign. A dozen other reporters came up too. McCarthy didn't know quite what to say for a minute. The kids in the audience didn't know what was going on except confusion. After a bit, McCarthy went back to the microphone and said he'd just been told Johnson had dropped out of the campaign. To the college kids, LBJ was the villain of Vietnam, and they cheered a lot. McCarthy said he didn't think he'd give any more speech. He went back to his hotel and I grabbed a telephone to file on what had happened. After I did the story on McCarthy's reaction—what there was of it—I called Bell, who was in the Milwaukee bureau at the time, and told him he ought to try to get more from

McCarthy at his hotel, since I'd be a while getting back
to the city.

"The hell with McCarthy," Jack said. "I'm getting
hold of Hubert Humphrey." That instant analysis was
dead right. McCarthy was an interesting sidelight, but
with LBJ out, Humphrey was going to be the
Democratic presidential nominee.

CHANCELLOR: In 1981, when high interest rates were much
in the news, I found myself on the air explaining, time
after time, the effect big federal deficits have on interest
rates. When the government goes in the red, it has to
borrow money, like any other organization. When it is
forced to borrow billions and billions of dollars, that
increases the demand for money, which pushes the
rates even higher. That's not news, and it is not some
arcane piece of economic information, but a lot of
people hadn't made the connection. Once it was pointed
out to them, they understood the day's news better, and
I had done my job better. That kind of analysis is
really a form of teaching.

MEARS: That's the kind I find most useful to read and most
satisfying to write. I don't believe many people read all
the way through a piece that tells them what to think.
I know I don't. But I do read the piece that explains
and helps me to understand. We've both said it, but it
bears repeating that what has gone before is a valuable
guide to what is happening now, and to why. The
President decides that there are too many news leaks
from his administration and that he is going to plug
them. People in the news business talk as though the
sky were falling. Well, I can remember writing a story
after Lyndon B. Johnson decided the same thing and
had all the public relations people in his administration
summoned to the White House to be lectured on the

subject. They came, listened, went away, and everything continued as before. Right after Ronald Reagan decided to plug the leaks, he gave his State of the Union address to Congress—and every substantive proposal had leaked into print, in detail, before he spoke. It's useful to put things like that into context. Even comforting.

CHANCELLOR: There are times in broadcast analysis when the right thing to do is to say nothing, to skip the analysis. I remember the night before President Nixon resigned. He went on television to tell the country of his decision, and I suppose it was the most nerve-racking and emotional evening any of us had spent in our professional careers. It was my job at NBC to come on when he finished, and while he was talking I kept thinking, What the hell am I going to say when he's done? What could possibly be said at a time like that?

And when the red light came on, I looked into the camera and said one word. I said, with a sort of sigh of relief, "Well." I paused for a couple of seconds, and then, in a very businesslike way, got on with the rest of the coverage that we had planned. It was the best thing I could have done. The people watching didn't need some guy like me to tell them what they'd just seen, or what a historic occasion it was. They knew that. Knowing when to shut up is sometimes as important as knowing when to talk.

6 *WORDS*

WEBSTER'S *Third New International Dictionary* boasts that it has "over 460,000 entries." In other words, words. On any given day, a reporter will need only 500 or 1,000 of them. The trick is to find the right ones, and to use them with precision.

The writer who put that statement on the dictionary jacket was correct, but not precise. The primary meaning of "over," according to the entry on page 1605, is "higher up than and usually directly above another object." It expresses relationships in space. "More than" is one of the subordinate definitions.

Either way, the reader gets the idea. But one is precise, and the other is not.

There is no shortage of rulebooks on usage and style. The classic is *The Elements of Style,* by William Strunk, Jr., and E. B. White. They conclude with this sound advice.

The language is perpetually in flux; it is a living stream, shifting, changing, receiving new strength from a thousand tributaries, losing old forms in the backwaters of time. To suggest that a young writer not swim in the main stream of this turbulence would be foolish indeed, and such is not the intent of these cautionary remarks.

The intent is to suggest that in choosing between the formal and the informal, the regular and the offbeat, the general and the special, the orthodox and the heretical, the beginner err on the side of conservatism, on the side of established usage.

It is not a matter of absolute rights and wrongs, or of slavish obedience to the established way of expressing ideas and imparting information. But the story written with precision and care is the story most likely to be read that way. Make a silly mistake in the use of a word, and the reader—many readers— will spot it and conclude that the reporter doesn't know what he's writing about. If something so easily checked as the use of a word is wrong, it can make a story suspect. After all, the facts are far more difficult to verify. They aren't in the dictionary.

This isn't another rulebook, but here's that rule again: Look it up. Look up words even when you are certain of their meaning. Often you will find implications you do not intend to impart, and synonyms that will tell the story more precisely.

There is, for example, a standard cop-out for writers who are not quite sure of what they're stating. It is the word "apparent." The word turns up frequently in stories about elections still in the counting process. "Harvey D. Harvey apparently was elected to Congress," the lead will say. The intent is to say that Harvey is so far ahead as to indicate that he has won the election, but maybe he'll lose when all the votes are counted. It is a common way around the dilemma of going to press with a story that doesn't say flatly who is going to Congress. Editors let it be written every election night.

It really doesn't do any good. No reader is going to forgive a reporter who elects the wrong candidate just because he hedged it with the word "apparent." Besides, the primary meaning of the word "apparent" is exactly the opposite of what is intended when it is used to indicate uncertainty. The definition is "readily seen, evident, obvious." The definition that makes "apparent" a hedge—"appearing or seeming to be"—comes lower on the list of meanings.

Both of us have used "apparent" as a qualifier to hedge stories about the outcome of contested events. Nobody's perfect.

The device is one to avoid. Better to state facts and let them speak than to render a judgment that really isn't a judgment at all. Write that Harvey D. Harvey was far ahead with 70 percent of the vote counted. Or write that he won.

But don't try to have it both ways, or one day you'll be wrong.

No book, no lecture, no irate editor, will make a newswriter so sensitive to the need for precision in wording as will one stupid mistake, out there in print for all the world to see and sneer.

MEARS: Thirty years ago, as a college sportswriter, I tried to get fancy without benefit of the dictionary and managed to use the word "maudlin" when I meant "mundane." It would have taken one minute to check the dictionary. That malaprop cost me a week of needling, but it taught me a lesson. I don't use words unless I'm positive, and sometimes I look them up even then.

CHANCELLOR: I use dictionaries more today than I did when I began. Sometimes, when I'm writing, I use a word and then check it out to see if I've got it right, and about one time in ten I change it. Dictionaries are useful for synonyms, as well. Half the time the synonym for the word I've looked up does a better job in the sentence. And for me, pronunciations are important. For years, I've been saying "Ah-*till*-a the Hun." Not long ago a dictionary informed me that it's

"*At*-ill-a." I've won enough bets on that one to buy another dictionary. I've now got nine.

The King's English means standard and correct usage. Don't mistake that for the President's English. Dwight D. Eisenhower wandered around the language in a manner that obfuscated (obscured) meaning. Politicians do that, often on purpose. It keeps them from being cornered.

Sometimes Presidents just speak incorrectly. As, for example, Jimmy Carter on nationwide television:

"The government of Iran must realize that it cannot flaunt with impunity the expressed will and law of the world community."

To flaunt is to show off. He meant "flout," which is to mock or scorn.

The mistake is common, in print and out.

Fuzzy or incorrect wording is not a partisan matter. Bill Safire of the *Times,* word sentry as well as columnist, caught President Reagan at it, and told on him. "I can assure you that by morning I'll be hung in effigy," Reagan said after proposing big cuts in the federal budget. Pictures are hung, Safire noted. Politicians are hanged, usually in effigy.

That's not to suggest that newswriters should clean up the syntax of politicians or anybody else. The job is to quote them accurately. But don't make their errors your own by using them in paraphrase, outside the quotation marks. That can be a challenge. Senator Edward M. Kennedy is capable of uttering sentences that run on and on, sometimes completely innocent of verbs. They don't really become full sentences, they just taper away. Here's Kennedy in a 1979 interview with Roger Mudd on what would have seemed the simple question of why he wanted to be president:

Well, I'm, were I to, to make the announcement and to run, the reasons that I would run is because I have a great belief in this country, and it—has more natural resources than any other nation in the world, has the greatest educated population in the world, the greatest technology of any country in the world, the greatest capacity for innovation in the world, and the greatest political system in the world. And yet, I see at the current time that most of the industrial nations of the world are exceeding us in terms of productivity, are doing better than us in terms of meeting the problems of inflation, that they're dealing with their problems of energy and their problems of unemployment. And it just seems to me that this nation can cope and deal with its problems in a way that it has in the past. . . . And I would basically feel that, that it's imperative for this country to either move forward, that it can't stand still, or otherwise it moves back.

The writer has not been born who could find the lead, or much sense, in that. Since that was a television interview, it ran as he said it, and did him no good in the campaign that followed. That probably would not have happened if he had said the same thing to a print reporter, since the answer was that he didn't say, and the answer defied paraphrase. That's a failing; better to spend some words to show that on so central a question, the candidate had no clear reply.

Politicians also have invented a new set of verbs that really are nouns. It is a tortured, silly language. As secretary of state, Alexander M. Haig, Jr., delivered himself of a new vocabulary. When a message was supposed to imply something without stating it directly, Haig said it was "nuanced" for the purpose. That sort of thing belongs in copy only in quotation marks. There is an ample supply of real words to tell any story. No need to invent new ones.

Nevertheless, the news business has coined its share of dreadful nonwords. Take "downplay," for example. It is the backward composite of "play down," a perfectly useful phrase. It turns up regularly in news copy. As in: "The administration today sought to downplay U.S. concern with the conflict in El Salvador."

Not even the unabridged has room for that hybrid. It does

not save space, it does not save words, and it ought to be banned.

It is a message word, the kind editors use in cables to their correspondents. It is still the lingo of wire service messages. "Locals downplaying crisis," one bureau will say in a message to another. That means the newspapers are not making prominent use of stories about the crisis. It is shorthand, code.

It is from the same stable as "upfollow," "downhold," and "soonest." "Upfollow" means to get to work matching a story or pursuing details for further stories on a subject. "Downhold" is the dread code word that means cut your expenses to the bone. "Soonest" means in a hurry.

In the real world, those words don't exist. Other combination words, like "upcoming" and "ongoing," do exist. But they've never done a thing for anybody's copy.

There are better ways to say what you mean. If something is going to happen soon, say that. A coming event gains no added import because a writer decides to make it an upcoming event. A situation is a situation. There's no need to clutter the sentence by calling it an ongoing situation.

Leave the language of the bureaucrats to the bureaucrats. Let them say "implemented." Newswriters can tell it better with a phrase such as "put into effect." Bureaucrats talk of "parameters" of a situation when they mean the limits. They like to "interface," which sounds like great fun but doesn't carry the meaning as well as a simple word like "relate."

The unfortunate habit, especially in Washington, is to slip into a jargon that makes things sound pretentious instead of simple. Complicated pronouncements seem more important than plain ones. But all they do is confuse readers and obscure meanings. The best writing provides translations, not jargon.

When there is a quorum call in the House or the Senate, what they are doing is taking attendance. Say so. When legislatures adjourn sine die, or prorogue, they end their sessions. Say so.

Most people think that "prorogue" has something to do with Cajun canoes.

It takes a few more words to explain technical phrases and jargon, or to provide background. But they are words well spent. It is not sinful to pause in presenting the latest set of developments in order to explain what has gone before. The customary way is to attempt that in shorthand, with a word or two, a phrase of background rationed out along with the new information.

Sometimes that works. More frequently, newswriters just pretend it works.

"My theory is that news people—the pros—don't read news copy the way ordinary mortals do," writes Charles R. Seib, former managing editor of the Washington *Star* and later ombudsman for the Washington *Post.*

> Because they know how it is constructed and because they usually are familiar with the context, they read it as a code.
>
> They jump agilely from element to element, from fact to fact, unhindered by the underbrush, unfatigued by the length of the journey. . . .
>
> There is a tradition that the story must move forward with every sentence. Otherwise, it is thought, the reader will desert it. It must have pace, we say. At the same time, we recognize that the reader must be provided with the background he needs to understand the latest developments. Stopping to give background in a straightforward way would interrupt that precious pace. So we ladle out the background in long dependent clauses that often push the predicate over the horizon from the subject.

Seib thinks that journalists recognize this technique and so can read past the clause of background to the active part of the sentence without losing track of the substance. He doesn't think the average reader can or does.

Some words are strained by overwork, used almost to the point of uselessness. They become trite because newswriters use them again and again. Habit and headline use combine to make them part of too many leads—some of our own included. The word "vow" is a sample. It is short, handy for the headline writer, and used to death. A vow is a solemn promise, especially one made to God. But every day, you'll find politicians vowing to win, prosecutors vowing to gain convictions, presidents vowing to get their programs enacted. A vow is not a glib political forecast. It is more serious than that. But it is probably too far gone to be saved.

Not that there is anything wrong with keeping the headline writer in mind when you write a story. The editor who puts the head on the copy has to count every space to make it fit. It is good discipline to think of that in choosing the words you use. Short, punchy words are almost always better than long, complicated words.

Reserve the longer, more ornate words for special situations, and they will mean more when you use them. For example, when the American hostages were released by Iran at the hour of Ronald Reagan's inauguration, it was time for words like "delivered from bondage."

Numbers are expressed in words too. But many a newswriter has bent sentences out of shape to avoid beginning with a number that has to be spelled out. There is nothing wrong with a precise number at the beginning of a sentence, not if it is important. If the thought flows with a number up front, write it that way. And don't use the dodge that puts an extraneous word first in order to avoid starting with a number. That way lies such foolishness as "Some 52 American hostages . . ." There were exactly 52 hostages.

It is common, and jarring, to see approximation words such as "some," "about," and "nearly" modifying numbers that are precise. There are few things sillier than a story that says: "The City Council approved *about* $3,247,143 for highway repairs today." But it is done, even by reporters who have taken the time to get the precise number.

Three million, two hundred and forty-seven thousand, one hundred and forty-three dollars is more than a mouthful for a broadcast reporter. In radio and television, numbers like that are rounded, and that one would be described as "almost three and a quarter million dollars."

The use of decimal points in numbers bears watching. If a legislature voted 3.7 million dollars for its own expenses, you probably wouldn't say to a friend, "It's going to cost three-point-seven million dollars." The decimal description of amounts of money is a useful form of shorthand in print and headlines, but in broadcasting it sounds stilted.

The news deals with ever larger amounts of money. The Reagan administration took office in 1981 with plans for 1.6 trillion dollars in additional defense spending. That, as Daddy Warbucks might have said, is quite a lot of money. Broadcast copy offers an opportunity to let the weight of all that money sink in. Instead of 1.6 trillion dollars say "one trillion six hundred billion dollars."

Precision makes better writing and more believable stories. It tells the reader that you did look it up, you did check it out. If it happened before, say so, and when—on December 13, 1969. It takes a few minutes to find out and a few words to say it. Both are worthwhile.

Sometimes there'll be a gift word that helps to tell the story better than any the reporter-writer can find. Grab it. When Richard Nixon used the word "crook" to deny that he was one, the story was made. But writers sometimes turn away from gifts like that, thinking to tell it in words of their choosing. Convention, and plain stubbornness, point that way.

When Prince Charles married Lady Diana Spencer, even the cynical found themselves watching the show. The story was compelling not because a prince with big ears was marrying a pretty lady. It was a worldwide audience of people who grew up on princes and princesses, on the Brothers Grimm, Hans Christian Andersen and the changing of the guard at Buckingham Palace. She was Cinderella and maybe he used to be a frog before she kissed him. It was a news story about childhood tales shared the world over.

The Archbishop of Canterbury provided the gift word in his sermon. It was, he said, the stuff of which fairy tales are made. There could be no better way to tell it. That was a line to seize. But many of the people who wrote the story thought to improve upon it. They produced copy reporting that Charles and Diana were married amid pomp and ceremony and parades and celebration. One writer ventured that they had wed to the cheers of British hearts, an interesting concept. It wasn't pomp and pageantry that drew the worldwide audience. It was those shared fairy tales.

Usually—almost invariably—stories like royal weddings, presidential inaugurations, parades and like ceremonies unfold according to script, and could be written before they happen. The challenge is to find the touches, and the words, that set it apart, give the predictable event a special flavor.

All ceremonies of state are conducted with pomp and the trappings of tradition. Those words are as predictable as a sunrise. They produce stories that could be filed away and dusted off every time whatever is happening happens. The only trouble is that they are old stories. Look for new angles, new ways to tell them.

MEARS: One of those set pieces happens on the final night of every national political convention. The nominees for President and Vice-President give their acceptance speeches. And a lot of us file dutiful, straight-faced reports which read: Richard M. Nixon accepted the Republican presidential nomination tonight. Change name and party and fill in the blanks. It happens twice every fourth year.

Writing it that way disregards the fact that Nixon or

Johnson, or Carter, or Ford, or Reagan, or whoever is accepting the nomination has spent millions of dollars, and about half his life, trying to get it. It's hardly news that he's decided to accept the thing. To make it even more predictable, nominees invariably accept nominations with humility and pride. They give every evidence of the latter, and none of the former.

I never have considered it to be news that a candidate who has just shaken his hand to the bone, and spent his family and friends to the poorhouse, in order to get the nomination has decided to accept same. When I write about those orations, I treat them as the first speech of the campaign. From that angle, there's news in them.

CHANCELLOR: There are times in broadcasting when formality and the predictable lead helps. Every presidential election night I prepare a paragraph or two on the candidates, which I put aside and use when we make our call on the winner. At a time like that, you don't want to ad-lib, because unless you're especially gifted, it comes out mushy. It's an important moment, involving our constitutional process. So I say: "We project, as the winner of the presidential election, John Wilson Brown [give the full name], fifty-seven years old, of Ohio [mention the state—we live in the United States], a farmer, businessman and governor, of the Baptist faith, a graduate of Ohio State University, who served in the army with the rank of colonel in the Vietnam war, married to the former Frances Anderson of Topeka, Kansas, father of Michael, Thomas and Susan."

I usually have similar copy ready for the inauguration. Such a moment requires formal copy. And the language should be spare. Save the stuff about how many times he tried, or how hard he worked, or the slogan which won him the job. Use it later.

Newswriting abounds in useless modifiers. Beware the extra word. Don't use it unless it adds something to the meaning of the sentence.

"Viable candidate," for example. Taken literally, that means that the candidate has developed sufficiently to live outside the womb. It is best not to bet money on candidates who have not developed to that point. We write viable candidate to mean a candidate who stands a chance of winning. Call the candidate a candidate, and if he is a guaranteed loser, take a few more words and explain why he doesn't have a chance. Be careful. Every once in a while, candidates who do not have a chance turn out to be the winners.

"Delicate surgery" is another cliché combination. If the surgery is not delicate, the surgeon is overpaid. Surgery is surgery, and should not be performed without some delicacy. A tonsillectomy is not as complicated as a heart transplant. Just report why the patient is under the knife.

"Successfully captured" and "long tradition" come from the same family of combinations that are redundant at worst and pointless at best.

Some words are misused so often that even editors come to accept them and send them on their errant way to print. "Refuted" is one of those. As in Senator So-and-so today refuted criticism of his voting record. He didn't refute it unless he proved it wrong. He probably couldn't do that on a bet. What the good senator did was rebut, or dispute, the criticism.

One word, especially one verb, can change the meaning or alter the tone of a story. That is one of the joys of writing. It also is one of the sorrows for the writer who lets it happen by accident.

For example, when U.S. Navy fighters shot down two Libyan

jets in 1981, Ronald Reagan's White House staff didn't tell him about it for six hours, until he'd slept most of the night. Reagan said they were right in not waking him. Cartoonists, stand-up comedians and columnists—who have more in common than they want to admit—had material for a week.

It was not a simple situation. Reagan's subsequent endorsement of bedtime notwithstanding, it was not the President who decided against a wee-hours briefing on the conflict. His aides made that decision. Tempting as it was, it really wasn't quite fair to use words that implied Reagan decided to sleep it out.

One story said that the President slumbered while the administration dealt with the clash. That is literally true. He did. But the inference of the verb is that he decided to slumber, and leave the mini-crisis to his aides. The straight way to tell it was that Reagan was not advised of the encounter for more than six hours.

Attribution verbs can be troublesome too.

It bears repeating that "said" is the handiest word in the language. It usually beats declared, claimed, contended, asserted, alleged, promised, and all the others.

It is a colorless word. Use it unless you mean to color the statement that follows—and can show in writing that the slant is accurate.

Substitute "claimed" for "said," and the verb casts doubt on the statement being quoted. Substitute "declared," and you may have elevated the statement, perhaps more than you intended. "Declared" is overused, and should be saved for formal statements and occasions.

Some stories slip past "said" with another verb. For example: "The President today deplored Soviet inroads into the Middle East." Presumably, he deplored them yesterday and will tomorrow. What he did today was to say that he deplored them.

Or: "The governor showed little concern about unrest at the state prison." That can be unfair. If he said he isn't concerned, write it that way. Perhaps he went about his day's routine and didn't say anything at all. Say what he said. Or say that he didn't say, and went to the ball game. Enough said.

Verbs can be character assassins. Unless it is the specific or accurate word, don't write that someone admitted, insisted, argued. Those are valuable words, but they've got to be kept in their place. Otherwise you risk unconsciously slanting the story.

Some writers get in trouble because of what the late Theodore Bernstein of the New York *Times* called monologophobia. That means a fear of using the same word more than once in a few sentences. Monologophobes use the word "say" in the first sentence, and then search desperately for an equivalent in the next. That can lead to the kind of paragraph in which an innocent official starts out by saying something, goes on to insist on it, and ends up admitting it—all because a writer didn't want to repeat the word "say."

This fear of repetition shows up in other ways. For example, a lead might report: "The government of Poland today announced plans to reform that country's economy." No repetition there. But there is nothing wrong with writing: "to reform the Polish economy." Too many writers are afraid of the repetition, and shove in "that country" instead. A better lead would be: "The government of Poland today announced plans for economic reform." The Polish government is not likely to announce plans to reform the economy of some other country.

Sportswriters are often incurably addicted to monologophobia; theirs is a craft in which there seem to be endless substitutions for "hit," or "win." But all writers are affected by it, possibly because they are taught when young that it's against the rules to use the same word twice in a sentence. It's not bad guidance, but it can be taken to extremes. Harold Evans, the distinguished British editor, observed that if such a rule had been followed by the writers of the Bible, part of the Book of Genesis would read: "Let there be light and there was solar illumination."

Quotations demand special care in broadcasting. If an opponent of the defense spending plan were to make a speech saying, "We are bankrupting the United States in order to save it," that comment, standing alone, might provide a lead for the written story. The attribution could follow.

It would be a bad lead for radio or television. Never begin a story with a quotation in broadcast writing. It confuses the audience, especially if it is a catchy quote. The listener or viewer hears it, and immediately asks, "Is the broadcaster saying that?" Nixon's "I am not a crook" was a remarkable and so newsworthy declaration, but in a newscast it had to be preceded by the words: "President Nixon said today . . ."

CHANCELLOR: Quotes in print are easy. In broadcasting, listeners need all the help they can get. When I am reading copy with quotations in it, I always make sure the viewer knows the words are not mine. I say, "Senator Moynihan said, quote," or I say, "In the senator's words . . ."

Saying "end quote" is often awkward. At the end of a quotation I try to begin a new paragraph or a new thought so the audience knows it is back with my words. Pausing—and on TV, looking down at the quotation—is helpful. The main point is to make clear that you are quoting someone else.

Words are wonderful things, but they have to be watched at all times, or they will turn on you. One of them can sneak out of line and do damage. A television series was once described as having as its central characters an "undercover rock group working to help the police." Maybe undercover rock is a new form of music. Or maybe the writer meant a rock group working under cover for the cops. That word got out of line.

Don't get carried away. A reporter in the Middle East once wrote of the late Anwar Sadat of Egypt that "a hesitant smile formed below his mustache." Had it formed elsewhere, it could have been some story.

And remember the basics. Harold Evans, in his book *Newsman's English,* reprints a set of "un-rules" from the *Rocky Mountain News:*

1. Don't use no double negative.
2. Make each pronoun agree with their antecedent.
3. Join clauses good, like a conjunction should.
4. About them sentence fragments.
5. When dangling, watch your participles.
6. Verbs has to agree with their subjects.
7. Just between you and I, case is important too.
8. Don't write run-on sentences they are hard to read.
9. Don't use commas, which aren't necessary.
10. Try to not ever split infinitives.
11. It's important to use your apostrophe's correctly.
12. Proofread your writing to see if you any words out.
13. Correct spelling is esential.

7 *SOURCES*

I̶n the beginning, there has to be a source—and that simple fact has created some of the most tortured language and logic in the news business. The informed source and the unimpeachable source are two prime players. The source on which any story is hung had better be both. That's so whether the information comes from someone who is identified or someone who insists on remaining anonymous. Go with an uninformed source, or an impeachable one, and you won't go far.

Actually, sources and sourcing are not nearly as mysterious as they've been made to sound. The story based on information obtained from an official who won't allow his name to be used is the exception, not the rule. For most stories, the source is the reporter, and what he has seen, or heard, or read. The quotations are attributed, the documents identified. And if you saw the building collapse, you don't have to attribute that to somebody else.

The most common sourcing in any newspaper is mundane and two words long: police said. There are jokes in the business that you can write almost anything and get it past the editors so long as it is tagged with those two words. As in: "The sky is falling, police said."

It isn't, of course, and if the police say it's falling, they are wrong. That is one of the problems with sourcing in any kind of reporting. The fact that someone in authority says something doesn't make it so. An unsubstantiated accusation or assertion is no less irresponsible for the fact that it comes from a person who holds office. Use your sources, but don't let them use you. Observation, an extra telephone call or two, and simple common sense can save a lot of grief.

Journalists like to talk about the public's right to know. There is some dispute about how much the public has a right to know, but there is one area of journalism about which there can be no dispute: the public has a right to know where we're getting the stuff we put into the papers and on the air, by name when possible, by description when necessary.

Journalism is the craft of telling what happened. Telling what happened requires the journalist to tell how the information was gathered, whether it was the announcement of the church supper or the leak from the Pentagon.

Who told you? How do you know? How reliable is the source? Is the source trying to peddle a point of view, to build up, or knock down, someone or something? Those are basic questions to be answered in any news story. If the answers aren't given, people have a right to gripe.

If it's a two-alarm fire of suspicious origin, make sure the suspicion is attributed to a real person, with credentials sufficient to have a suspicion. Better when that person has a title, an official position, and a middle initial. A reporter has a right to suspicions, but no license to write them. It isn't necessary to attribute plain fact—the height of the skyscraper, the score of the ball game. But never make an assertion in a news story without giving the reader or viewer knowledge of where that assertion came from.

If senior officials of the U.S. government are considering a new kind of intercontinental missile, but don't want their names used, the reporter has some decisions to make. Is the information real—a coming change in policy and weaponry? Or is it a leak by one side in a divided administration, calculated to influence policy and alter the outcome? Either way it is a story, but it will take some checking to find out which story.

When that story is written, it must include the fact that the officials insisted on remaining anonymous, and it should tell as much as possible about their credentials. Are they hawks or doves? Civilian or military? Air force or navy?

Nothing is leaked to a reporter without a reason. The reason sometimes is as important as the leaked information.

The debate about unidentified sources is as old as the business. Unless you find a whistle-blower or a bureaucratic malcontent who doesn't care about his job, officials who provide information before their bosses want it known are going to insist that their identities be withheld and protected.

Sometimes they'll provide information their bosses do want out, anonymously. There is always the risk of being used that way by a politician or an official. Sometimes they just want to feel important, and there are journalists who assist. "Informed sources" has an omniscient ring. It makes it sound as though the writer knows things not available to ordinary mortals, and some newspeople prefer it that way. Don't join them.

There is a certain mystique about the unidentified source. It suggests the reporter is in the know, a confidant of well-placed officials and senior members of Congress. Frankly, it also makes it sound as though the story was more difficult to obtain than one in which an official makes known information directly, and with attribution.

It is really the other way around. Senior officials are not hard to find, so long as they are allowed to speak for print without real identification. The challenge is to find someone in authority who is willing to put a name behind the information.

Years ago, the boss of the AP bureau in Washington laid down a strange law against unidentified sources. He made up a name for them, and ordered it used. Whenever there was a story citing a source that was not identified, the information was to be attributed to a figment called "D. C. Speaker." As in: "The President has decided not to run again, D. C. Speaker said today." The rule didn't last long. Editors got to wondering who in the world D. C. Speaker might be, and how he could possibly be so knowledgeable on so much.

MEARS: When Barry Goldwater was running for President, he kept getting into trouble over statements he made in response to questions, on his chartered airplane or at news conferences. His imagemakers decreed that there would be no more comments on the record—it would all be background. Goldwater would hold what amounted to an airborne news conference, but what he said could be attributed only to "sources" close to the candidate. I was one of the junior political reporters on that campaign. I argued that the tactic was out of bounds for any candidate, let alone a presidential candidate. Some of the senior men passed the word that I should shut up. After all, there are more columns to be had in background information than in on-the-record statements by the Republican presidential nominee. So the rule stood. The elders got their columns, and I refused to write anything Goldwater wouldn't put on the record. AP backed me up, even though we forfeited some play to stories that had the mysterious source on the airplane making charges against the Democrats.

There are legitimate situations in which the only way to get a story is to withhold the identity of the source. That happens most frequently in Washington, but it happens at the state house and city hall too. To get information, a reporter has to agree to write it without naming the source. Resist that when you can, but if the information is important, there'll be times when you'll have to agree on anonymity for the source—and take the risks that go with it. Officials have been known to deny stories they planted themselves.

The value of the information has to be weighed against the risks inherent in using it without identifiable attribution. It is a judgment call, and a reporter can get burned. After he's been burned a few times, the judgment and the handling get better than they were first time out.

The starting-point rule is to go with unidentified sources when they are the only way to get at information. But use them only on matters of fact. No one should be allowed to express opinion or make judgments in your copy without putting a name behind the views.

If an official tells you, "Here's what I think about Cuba, but don't use my name," tell him to forget it. But if he tells you, "Here's what the administration is going to do about Cuba," listen, weigh it, check it out if you can, and decide whether to write it.

Frequently the most colorful quotes available will be blind quotes—that is, statements by people who don't want to be identified. Congressmen, mayors, businessmen and, for that matter, newspeople are most likely to let the vitriol flow after insisting that their names not be published. Don't use blind quotes unless they impart facts. If somebody in authority wants to say that the county assessor doesn't know what he's doing, let him say it and put his name with it. Should the same official show up with documentary proof that real estate assessments are inaccurate, you've got facts that are worth writing, with attribution if possible, with an unidentified source if necessary.

Precision in sourcing and identification applies to all levels of newswriting. If police say (there's that phrase again) that a man named Waldorf Tattinger has been caught in a raid on a whorehouse, be damned sure he is precisely identified. If Waldorf B. Tattinger of 124 South Main Street is the man, write it that way and attribute the identification to the police, or the district attorney. That way, Waldorf G. Tattinger of 334 North Main Street won't come at you with a libel suit or a bullwhip.

Sometimes you can't provide identifications. If anyone vulnerable to publicity is involved, go carefully. State and local laws vary on publication of the names of victims, and of youthful offenders. The policies of news desks vary too. Those policies should protect the identities of people who might be endangered or victims who would be humiliated if names were used.

This applies to the relatives of people in the news. The brother of the child molester leads a blameless life. His name and address don't belong in print. Put them there, and he's harmed.

A news story can be studded with facts, middle initials, ages, addresses, occupations, and still be incomplete if a centrally important fact is stuck in without attribution. Who said that the defendant was hiring out-of-town lawyers? How did the reporter learn that the candidate had been in a mental institution?

Even when you've got them on the record, take care with the statements of officials and other people cited in the story. The police captain may say proudly that the "street value" of the heroin confiscated in the raid is several million dollars. Street value is a lot more than the drug peddlers paid for the stuff; it's a theoretical number representing what addicts might pay for it in the end. But it makes drug busts sound more impressive. When the police give you their figure on the value of the dope, ask the feds. Or vice versa. Then quote them by name and position.

As a rule, when a policeman, a politician or an official says something that makes him or her look smart, hard-working, clever or heroic, get to work on checking it out. That's one of the things good sourcing is all about.

Good reporters know that there are dozens of facts about people and their transactions listed in public records, and many stories are enriched by these facts. It is important, however, to say where you got them.

You can write that a man charged with drunken driving has been convicted twice on hit-and-run charges. But go on to say that is according to records at the county courthouse. When it's a matter of public record, say so, and say where, and you'll have a better story. When it isn't public record, you probably won't be able to use it at all. And when somebody tells you it is on the public record, go and see for yourself.

There are times when self-serving officials will show reporters documents after obtaining a pledge that the names of the officials won't be used. Again, the caution light should flash. Why does an official show a reporter something? To make somebody look good—or to make somebody look bad. Suppose those hit-and-run convictions were in another state, and not on file down at the local courthouse? Why would an official insisting on anonymity show them to a journalist? The answer is obvious: to prejudice the case against the man charged with drunken driving.

In cases like these, the documents are useless unless the story says where they came from, and from whom. "Law enforcement officials" is one technique often used. "Sources close to the investigation" is another. Both are cop-outs which can get you into trouble—legal as well as journalistic trouble. The public has a right to know that the prosecutors are trying to prejudice the case. So does the defendant.

It's okay to use material like that when it is central to the story and when the copy states explicitly that the information was volunteered by police or prosecutors. In other words, they made sure you knew about it because they wanted you to write it. Names are best, but not always essential in this kind of sourcing. Most people don't know the names of the prosecutors, or policemen, anyway. Their motivation is important to the story. Facts are facts, but where they come from and why can be just as important as the information itself.

This is especially true in political reporting. If the mayor and the head of the board of education are enemies, or the governor and the senator, one side is likely to be telling reporters things about the other. The name-calling is a story in itself. And the feud can generate tips, information, worth checking with unbiased sources.

Often, partisans on one side in a political campaign will offer reporters poll information that makes their candidate look good, or damages the other one. A source like that is not doing you any favors; he's trying to do himself one. So be careful. Polls are hard to handle correctly under any circumstances. And the kind candidates or their managers try to float are suspect. Often, they'll tell part of the story and skip the part that does not look good for their side. In presidential primary election campaigns, candidates sometimes will try to float polls showing they're behind, so as to lower expectations and enhance their showings when the votes are counted. Losing the New Hampshire primary isn't so damaging for a candidate who has managed to convince people he shouldn't be expected to do well there. Winning by a smaller-than-expected margin can be a setback for the favorite; it was for Lyndon Johnson in 1968 and for Edmund Muskie in 1972.

When polling information is going to be used, the story has to identify the side that provided the poll. It also needs to say how many people were polled, when, and exactly what they were asked. Anonymous reports of partial poll results are not worth writing; they are advertisements, not news.

Furthermore, the story needs to tell the reader why the figures were disclosed.

One of the landmark leaks in recent times took place when Daniel Ellsberg, a former government official, gave the "Pentagon Papers," as they came to be known, to the New York *Times* in 1971. It was a compilation of classified documents on the Vietnam war, and it led to a historic legal confrontation be-

tween the press and the Nixon administration, which wanted
the stories suppressed.

Here's how the *Times* first reported the story:

> A massive study of how the United States went to war in Indo-
> china, conducted by the Pentagon three years ago, demonstrates
> that four administrations progressively developed a sense of com-
> mitment to a non-Communist Vietnam, a readiness to fight the
> North to protect the South, and an ultimate frustration with this
> effort—to a much greater extent than their public statements ac-
> knowledged at the time.
>
> The 3,000-page analysis, to which 4,000 pages are appended, was
> commissioned by Secretary of Defense Robert S. McNamara and
> covers the American involvement in Southeast Asia from World
> War II to mid-1968—the start of the peace talks.

That was the first installment in the *Times,* and it did not give
a source. The *Times* had the documents, and didn't say where
they came from, only that they were authentic.

Sourcing aside, the *Times* story, and those that followed it,
led to one of the great constitutional struggles between press
and government. Here were forty-seven typescript volumes of
secret government documents, 2,500,000 classified words, and
the *Times* had them all.

Richard M. Nixon didn't know the Pentagon Papers existed
until Neil Sheehan's story was published in the *Times* on June
13, 1971. But he knew he didn't like secrets in the newspapers.

His Justice Department asked the *Times* to stop publishing
Pentagon Papers stories, citing espionage laws and saying that
the stories were damaging U.S. security. The *Times* reported
the request in the same edition that carried the third installment
of the Pentagon Papers story.

The government then went to court and got a temporary
order barring further publication. That silenced the *Times,* in
a way. But on the same day, the Washington *Post* began publishing its own stories on the documents. The *Post,* clearly, had

obtained a set of the papers too. Under court order against covering the story it had broken, the *Times* published Associated Press accounts of the material that was appearing in Washington, until the government got a restraining order against the *Post* as well.

The issue was drawn: Did the government, in peacetime, have a right to suppress material in advance of publication? It went quickly to the Supreme Court, which ruled on June 26 that the answer was no.

Meanwhile, the source surfaced in the person of Daniel Ellsberg. A fortnight after the first *Times* story appeared, he turned himself in to U.S. marshals in Boston. He had helped prepare the documents as an employee of Rand Corporation, a think tank contractor to the Pentagon. Once a hawk, he had become a dove, and said he could no longer cooperate in keeping the Pentagon Papers from the American people.

Ellsberg was indicted and tried, along with a former colleague. It was the first time Americans had been accused of espionage for releasing information to American newspapers.

The charges ultimately were dismissed. But the Pentagon Papers case was a way station on the path to an even more momentous case—Watergate. The administration's covert operations against Ellsberg, up to and including burglary, contributed to the attitudes and tactics that finally drove Nixon from the White House.

That story unfolded largely because of the work of two men and one newspaper, Robert Woodward, Carl Bernstein and the Washington *Post.* It raised the most complex and controversial sourcing problems newsmen and editors ever had faced. For they were publishing accusations of wrongdoing by the most powerful men in government and their sources were, of necessity, anonymous.

The best of those sources was the famous, still anonymous, "Deep Throat." The name became newsroom slang; they didn't put it in the paper. It was, after all, borrowed from the title of a pornographic movie.

For years, guessing about the identity of Deep Throat has been a Washington parlor game. Some people say the source was a single White House official, others that it described a group of people. Benjamin Bradlee, executive editor of the *Post,* said long after Watergate that Deep Throat was one person, and that he knew who it was. He never said who, nor did anyone else.

In their book *All the President's Men,* Woodward and Bernstein described the source, and the way his information was used:

> Woodward had a source in the executive branch who had access to information at the Committee for the Re-election of the President as well as at the White House. His identity was unknown to anyone else. He could be contacted only on very important occasions. Woodward had promised he would never identify him or his position to anyone. Further, he had agreed never to quote the man, even as an anonymous source. Their discussions would be only to confirm information that had been obtained elsewhere and to add some perspective.

The story began, of course, with the break-in and attempted bugging of Democratic party headquarters in the Watergate office building on June 17, 1972. It turned out that the raid had been financed with funds passed through Nixon's presidential campaign committee, but even then, the President's spokesman called it no more than a third-rate burglary attempt that did not and would not involve Nixon. It did, for it was only the tip of the story Woodward and Bernstein got from their confidential sources. There were secret slush funds, dirty tricks, attempts at political sabotage, illegal wiretaps. The major elements of that story unfolded as Woodward and Bernstein published the information they got from confidential sources. The descriptions of those sources were familiar ones. One story would cite "a source close to the federal investigation"; another, "an FBI source."

One major piece began this way:

> FBI agents have established that the Watergate bugging incident stemmed from a massive campaign of political spying and sabotage conducted on behalf of President Nixon's re-election and directed by officials of the White House and the Committee for the Re-election of the President.
>
> The activities, according to information in FBI and Department of Justice files, were aimed at all the major Democratic presidential contenders and—since 1971—represented a basic strategy of the Nixon re-election effort.

Woodward and Bernstein found and used multiple sources, sometimes as many as ten for one story, in order to expand and corroborate their information.

Eventually, as the story developed, official inquiries produced on-the-record information.

But that was after months of source stories, investigative pieces that pitted the two reporters and their newspaper against the power of an administration, all on the basis of informants who could not be publicly identified.

The stories were startling, but the description of their sources was familiar to every newsman. Woodward and Bernstein quoted sources in the Watergate bugging investigation, sources close to the investigation, well-placed sources in the White House and the Justice Department, informed sources, highly placed sources in the executive branch. Any experienced Washington newsman has used many of the same constructions; after all, nobody purposely quotes uninformed sources, or poorly placed ones. But never had such a sequence of source stories delivered information so damaging to officials so powerful.

The reaction was predictable. President Nixon's official and political spokesmen called it political garbage, unsubstantiated charges and hearsay information.

Day after day, the White House cried foul, issued denials and protested that the stories were based on anonymous sources. Other news organizations picked up summaries of what the *Post* had printed, and wrote their own stories, often featuring the White House denials. That's a standard way to match stories you don't have—let an official deny them on the record, and then write what it is that they're denying.

After all, the denials have a name behind them, and the investigative sources are anonymous. That is a route around the dilemma of a newsman who has been beaten on a story. But it creates an even greater dilemma when, as in Watergate, the sources delivered truth and the officials who could be identified were lying or ignorant of the facts they were denying.

(Politicians and presidents know the system—and use it. The process of matching somebody else's story is subject to manipulation. An official who plants—leaks—information in the right place can sit back and watch while the rest of the press catches up with the story. That keeps the leaker's story in print and on the air, sometimes for days.)

For all that, anonymous sources did not undo the President. The information Woodward and Bernstein wrung from them was a vital part of the process, but Nixon resigned because of what happened later, on the record, in courtrooms and in Congress. He might have survived Deep Throat; those accusations could be denied forever, or at least for the balance of his term in office.

Not so with the courtroom allegation of Watergate burglar James McCord that higher-ups had been involved in the plot, that perjury had been committed at the trial of the burglars, and that they had been pressured to plead guilty and remain silent to cover up for others.

Nor with the White House tapes or the testimony that unfolded in the Senate Watergate hearings; and later, in House impeachment proceedings against Nixon.

That is not to underestimate the role of the reporters; it does not diminish their achievements to acknowledge that in any investigative story there comes a point at which sources won't suffice. When that time came in Watergate, what Woodward and Bernstein had reported, and much more, was validated on the record.

The difficulty of Watergate sourcing stirred a controversy that hasn't gone away yet, even though the information Woodward and Bernstein obtained was proved, point by point. Conservative critics—and Richard Nixon still had his defenders— spent years demanding that the *Post* identify Deep Throat.

They renewed those demands with a vengeance after *Post* reporter Janet Cooke acknowledged that she had fabricated the story of an eight-year-old heroin addict for which she won a 1981 Pulitzer Prize. The *Post* returned the prize, and Miss Cooke resigned.

That episode stirred agonized debate throughout the business on the whole question of unidentified sources. Memos flowed, source policies were put into writing, and a good many editors said it couldn't have happened in their operation.

Unhappily, a good many editors probably were wrong. The Janet Cooke case did not involve unidentified sources. It involved the veracity of a reporter.

Had she written that a source insisting on anonymity had told her of an eight-year-old heroin addict, it would have triggered an entirely different kind of alarm system. An editor would have wanted to know the source. The information would have been checked with officials and other sources would have been sought.

But Cooke's was not a source story. It was, or purported to be, an eyewitness account by the journalist. Editors ask reporters all sorts of questions about their stories. But editors do not ask whether they made up the story. That is unthinkable, or was. It's happened on other papers since the Cooke episode, and it is menacing. If an editor can't trust his reporters not to write fiction, the news business can't function.

Those cases are aberrations. The source problem is eternal.

The Cooke story led to a season of soul-searching about sources, prompting author Tom Wolfe to write that he was amused at seeing it blamed on new trends in journalism:

When I arrived at the New York *Herald Tribune* in 1962, people were still talking about the great "Ship of Sin" scandal of Prohibition days. It seems the *Trib* had been informed that there was a ship operating off eastern Long Island, just beyond the three-mile limit, as a vice den of the high seas. The word was that this ship offered liquor, gambling and most known forms of sex. An investigative reporter (also nothing new) was sent to find the floating fleshpot, board her and bring the story back.

He was unable to find the ship, but he did find a saloon in Montauk, and he telephoned in a week's worth of the creamiest and most lurid chronicles in the annals of drunk newspapermen. The *Trib* couldn't print them fast enough. Half the city gasped; the other half headed for eastern Long Island to rent motor launches. When the hoax was revealed, the *Trib* fired the reporter, whereupon, legend has it, three other New York newspapers offered him jobs.

Maybe they did, but inventing stories, or any of the ingredients of stories, does not look good on the résumé. Serious journalism can function only when it produces information that is both true and trusted. When the information comes from sources that cannot be identified, it is up to the reporter to make sure they can be trusted to speak the truth.

Most reporters try to get the source to agree to some measure of identification ("a member of the hospital staff," "a relative," "a member of the jury," "an employee of the company"). In many cases, corroboration can be sought from other sources in a position to know. Then it's easy. A single source should make a reporter uneasy. Two are better. Three are better yet. Corroborating records or documents are best of all.

But what happens when there can be no corroboration? Gauge the quality of the source, if that's the case. Be wary of strangers. If the source is gold-plated and copper-bottomed, a trusted member of the community, with no obvious ax to grind, go with the story, and protect the source. If the source won't agree to any kind of personal description, try to use something about the source's own credentials ("someone who has seen the documents," "someone who has spoken with the accused").

That helps validate the information. Some of the old standbys don't help. "A source familiar with the case" doesn't tell enough when the source has a stake in the outcome of the case. Informed sources and reliable sources live on, in all their redundancy.

Unless the adjective imparts information, forget it. But if it is possible to ascribe information to a foreign diplomatic source, a military source, an administration source, then, at least, the description helps the reader weigh what the source disclosed.

Incidentally, all too often the plural "sources" is window dressing for a story with a single, unidentified source. If there is one source, the story should say so. Making the singular into the plural is flatly unethical.

Don't be casual with confidential sources. They can provide significant and interesting information, but they also can make a story suspect—and they can also send a reporter to jail. It has happened, and will again, when journalists refuse to tell judges where they got the story.

The city of Washington would go out of business if it weren't for anonymous sources. It is not only the capital of the United States; it is the world capital of "officials," "diplomats," "Senate staff members," "White House staffers," "National Security Council officials," "State Department officials," "Defense Department officials"—all talking to the press day after day, year after year, on the condition that their names not be used. Sometimes it gets to be kind of a joke.

Sometimes it's shorthand. It's easier to write "a Defense

Department official" than to write "the Assistant Deputy Under Secretary of Defense for Plans and Resources."

Sometimes it's required. Officials in Washington have created a set of rules of attribution designed to protect themselves while making it possible for whatever administration is in office to sell its particular brand of salami to the public.

There are four general categories of briefings for reporters, in groups or individually: on the record, background, deep background and off the record.

An official speaking on the record stands up, gives his name and allows himself to be directly quoted, filmed, taped, recorded and photographed. Presidential press conferences are on the record.

It hasn't always been that way. Franklin Delano Roosevelt held 998 press conferences, but he often spoke off the record, and he never could be quoted directly. Herbert Hoover had taken questions in writing; Roosevelt took them in person—and set down his rules at his first presidential press conference, on March 8, 1933.

"Straight news from this office should always be without direct quotation," he said. "Direct quotes must be in writing from Steve [Early, his press secretary]. Background information is not attributable to the White House."

Roosevelt also supplied a terse description of the news conference as a forum for the delivery of information—it was the President's show. And still is. "When anything is said," he told reporters to tell their editors, "it will be at a time of my choosing and not of their choosing."

Harry S. Truman operated under the Roosevelt rules, with periodic dispensations to permit direct quotation of segments he particularly liked. One was "red herring" as a description of Republican charges that his administration had been infiltrated by Communists.

In Dwight D. Eisenhower's White House, newsmen could report what the President said at a press conference but couldn't quote him directly until his answers had been transcribed and the transcripts distributed.

All of that changed when John F. Kennedy became President. He put the news conference on live television in 1961. From this time on, the formal presidential news conference was open to anyone with a television set or a radio and what was said was on the record, in the President's words, from the moment it was uttered. There was no longer any way to call back a misstatement. It had to be corrected—presidential spokesmen usually prefer to say "clarified"—after it had been broadcast.

"On the record" is the only variety of information that isn't subject to abuse.

Background briefings are those in which the official cannot be named, but his organization can be identified. That's the origin of stories attributed to "Defense Department officials," or "White House officials," or variations thereof.

The background briefing is supposed to give the briefer more latitude to "help" the reporter understand the story. State Department types hold them routinely, on grounds that they can speak more freely about foreign governments on background than on the record. It is hard to see why. The cover doesn't fool any foreign government.

Backgrounders have to be off camera. If television is there, it can't be background.

Some backgrounders do provide valuable information to help explain a government decision or action. Some are silly. Relatively minor government officials have been known to schedule briefings and announce after the reporters are there that the proceedings are on background. It seems to make them feel important. Even sillier, some of them have had their pictures taken, and printed in the paper, while speaking on background.

Background briefings are held in Washington almost every day, and their use is spreading across the country and around the world. It's a victory of bureaucracy over journalism, and journalism doesn't complain much.

Newspeople say they can't boycott backgrounders because the competition will be there and they'll be beaten on the story. And some—although they won't admit it—like writing about "government sources," because it sounds as though they're in the know.

Beyond the background briefing lies the dark and dismal swamp of deep background. The rules of deep background require the reporters to "know" things they can't attribute. Deep background is a favorite device of officials in the national security field, at the State and Defense Departments and at the White House. It produces such tortured attributions as "it is known." An official will say, "Let me put this on deep background," and the reporters dutifully print "DB" in their notebooks. The official will then say the Soviets have increased the number of SS-20 missiles deployed in Eastern Europe. This was learned through satellite reconnaissance, which is why the information can't be attributed to the United States government. The reporters are supposed to fold that information into their stories as though they owned the satellites. The fact that *(a)* the Soviets know how many missiles they have deployed, and that *(b)* they know the United States has seen them with its satellites is not considered relevant in deep background transactions.

A grand master of background, deep or otherwise, was Henry A. Kissinger, the former secretary of state. He flew around the world on background, a font of information that could be attributed only to "a senior official aboard the secretary's plane." Everybody knew it was Kissinger, but under the rules, the reporters couldn't say so. Sometimes Kissinger the secretary would deny what Kissinger the senior official had said the day before. The senior official was born Kissinger, but the cover lives under his successors.

The ultimate in attempted information control is "off the record." That means the information is not to be printed or broadcast. It can be useful: The White House Press Office can tell reporters that the President is planning an overnight trip to Canada, but that for reasons of protocol, the information can't be made public for a few days. The advance information is of value to reporters, however, in terms of relations with spouses, dinner engagements and when to take the car in for repairs.

Off the record has been used on a grand scale. During World War II, General George C. Marshall, top man in the American military, gave regular briefings to senior newspaper editors, columnists and broadcasters. Everything he said was off the record. But he said just about everything: He gave advance notice of invasions, he told of defeats and victories, he shared top-secret information with his audience of journalists, because he thought it would help in the coverage of the war effort. He was right. It helped. There was never a betrayal of his trust. But that was wartime, and a long time ago.

Sometimes, off the record is used as a device to keep information out of print. An official will exact a promise from a reporter that what he's about to be told will be off the record, and then the official will reveal something damaging to the administration. The reporter is stuck. He's promised not to use it, not from that source. He'll try to get it elsewhere. But off-the-record candor sometimes will buy the official some time to deal with the problem.

CHANCELLOR: Sometimes the off-the-record thing is just used foolishly. I remember being in Milwaukee on the eve of the 1980 Wisconsin primary. There was a lot about the American hostages in Iran in the news, and about Ayatollah Khomeini. There was a story around that President Carter had written a letter to the Ayatollah softening the American position on the hostages.

Well, the phone rang there in Milwaukee that afternoon and it was, guess who, the President himself on the line.

He said, "John, what I'm going to tell you is off the record."

I said, "Mr. President, I suspect what you're going to tell me involves Iran. We have a rule at NBC News that we won't accept off-the-record information if it's going to tie our hands in the coverage of a story. So I guess I can't hear what you've got to say."

There was a long pause. Then Mr. Carter said, "Well, I'll tell you anyway." He told me he hadn't softened his position on the hostages. That wasn't news.

MEARS: There's also a problem—even with Presidents—of getting the rules straight. When Carter was cultivating newsmen, I was at a small dinner party at which he said he was speaking on background. It was shortly before the fall of the Shah of Iran, and the President said the United States had offered him haven. He even said where—at the estate of Walter Annenberg in Palm Springs. Carter said some other things, stipulating that they were off the record. The next day, I assigned a reporter to look into the offer of haven (that's the word Carter used). Within an hour, I had a call from the White House. The aide who had arranged the dinner said the whole thing was supposed to be off the record. I pointed out that the President had called it background, and the aide said that was a mistake. We never were able to nail down a story, so it didn't get written.

One off-the-record champion was George Wallace, of Alabama, when he was running for President. You'd go into his office in Montgomery for an interview, and he would answer every question by repeating lines from public speeches, punctuating them by drawling, "That's off the record."

Most government officials, lawyers and diplomats know what it means to speak on background or off the record. But some of them throw the terms around because it sounds important. Where a savvy source will say to a reporter, "Look, you'll protect me on this, won't you?" an amateur will say, "Now, this has got to be off the record," even though his very purpose probably is to get the information into the paper or on the air. He just doesn't want his name used.

All too often, reporters create problems for themselves in this area. They do it by asking officials whether information at a briefing is for the record or for background. That's a mistake. It invites attribution problems. Assume that everything anyone says is on the record unless they stipulate otherwise. Don't get roped into background rules unless there's no other way to get the story.

And don't worry if your sources complain after the fact that they didn't understand they were going to be quoted by name. They know what you do for a living: write things down and put them in the paper.

Any official who doesn't understand that is too naive for his job.

The use of sources with no characterization at all can be a disservice. One of the worst offenders is the phrase "has learned," as in "The *Daily Eagle* has learned." An NBC correspondent once reported on trouble in an Israeli jail, and said: "NBC News has learned that the difficulty may have been caused by lawyers who have been allowed to visit Palestinian prisoners." Learned from whom? It's obvious that the lawyers didn't tell him that, so the jailers must have. Will an audience catch the distinction? Probably not. But the report that the Arab lawyers were causing the difficulties is given strength and credibility by the reporting. Much better to report that Israeli officials suspect the Arab lawyers.

That kind of phrasing is also pointless. If you hadn't learned it, how in the world could you report it? It is a self-important phrase that imparts no information.

For that matter, so is the "exclusive interview." A reporter's interview is by definition exclusive. If it's a group interview, say so.

Another old packhorse of a phrase that should be avoided is "observers noted." Observers have been noting for much of this century, and it's time to retire the phrase. What it often means is that the writer is the observer. Many news desks operate on the principle that nobody cares what the writer thinks, so writers turn to observers who are simply made up for the occasion. It may not hurt anyone, but it's a fake. A little extra effort can make the observation the observer observed newsworthy. It's wrong to say observers noted that candidate Jones has changed his position on abortion. The right way is to report that candidate Jones was saying something else last year. That's a fact which doesn't need an observer. Too often, the so-called observers are a disguise for the reporter's own opinion. The public deserves to be told if it's an opinion. Slipping it into the mouth of a nonexistent observer is cheating.

This kind of writing is not as pervasive as it used to be. But in the old days there were some wonderful examples of it. In a dispatch to the New York *Times* from Berlin in 1934, Frederick T. Birchall described a Nazi purge. In the fifth paragraph, he wrote: "There is mention of a 'foreign power' as being involved. The discerning interpret this reference as being to Russia."

The discerning? Wonderful. But not these days, thank you.

In political writing, there's always the mentioner: as in Senator So-and-so has been mentioned as a possible candidate for President. Just who does the mentioning never gets said. Usually it's the would-be candidate or his friends. And one mention is enough to get the prospective candidate on the list of regularly mentioned prospects.

There are occasions when proper sourcing acts as an insurance policy. In some broadcast newsrooms, there's a rule that if only one wire service has an important story, or a key quote, the wire service must be credited in the body of the story. This does two things: If the story is wrong, the mistake can be blamed on the wire service the next day; if the story is right, and exclusive, the wire service deserves the credit.

Anonymous sources can backfire on government. In his book *The Politics of Lying* (New York: Random House, 1973), David Wise tells the tale of how President Lyndon Johnson's desire to embarrass a reporter led to an international financial crisis.

The reporter was Douglas Kiker, now of NBC News, then the White House correspondent for the New York *Herald Tribune*. The year was 1965, and Johnson was recuperating from his gall bladder operation at his ranch in Texas. The White House press was quartered at the Driskill Hotel in Austin.

Johnson didn't like Douglas Kiker, and he devised a scheme to embarrass him. One week, when Kiker was at home in Washington, Johnson learned that the *Herald Tribune* was represented in Austin by a new man, named Richard Dougherty.

Johnson ordered the assistant White House press secretary to leak a story to Dougherty, believing that would diminish Kiker's standing at the paper. The President hoped that when Dougherty's exclusive appeared, the *Herald Tribune*'s editors would say that Kiker never got stories like that.

It wasn't much of a story. Johnson had summoned his chief economic advisers to the ranch. But at that time the consumer price index had just reached a record high. The combination of these two stories would backfire on LBJ.

The story about the economic advisers was leaked to Dougherty without attribution. At that point, things began to fall apart. Dougherty, who didn't think he had much of a story, told a colleague from the New York *Times* about the impending arrival of the economic advisers, and they both filed the story.

The *Times* put it on the front page, coupled with the bad news about consumer prices. The AP and UPI picked it up—not from the *Herald Tribune* but from the *Times*—and sent it out around the world. The story was played as though Johnson had panicked over the threat of inflation.

The stock market fell. The Federal Reserve Board acted to increase interest rates, which went up to the highest level in thirty years. There was talk of investigations in the Senate and the House.

All because Lyndon Johnson wanted to make Douglas Kiker look bad. And until years later, Kiker never knew anything about it.

Sometimes sources have to be disguised. Your source may have been among the two or three people in the room when an important decision was made, or on a limited-distribution list for documents. On occasions like these, the attribution of the story becomes deliberately vague. Whenever possible, the single source should be broadened. The original information can be used as a tip; try to find someone who can corroborate what you've got.

Investigative reporters take pieces of information and treat them as known fact when seeking corroboration. If the mayor has decided that the new airport will be located south of town, instead of north, others are learning of that decision. Call them and treat it as something that is being talked about. Ask a small question about the timing of the announcement, or what their reaction is, and you will often get confirmation. People are often, understandably, afraid to be the first with the news, but are usually willing to provide some corroborative details. After that, the sourcing is easy.

One way to use sources who won't be identified is as a tip service, a starting point. If an official tells you something off the record, it's a good bet that he's told other people on the record. Find them, and you've got a story you can write with authority.

Over a midnight drink in Williamsburg, Virginia, Vice-President Agnew told some reporters that he had reservations about his own administration's overtures to Communist China. It was in the days of ping-pong diplomacy, when an American team went to the mainland to bat the ball with a Chinese team. A curious opening, but the first flickering of the policy that became normalization.

What Agnew said was off the record. But he said it during a conference of Republican governors, and reporters who were bound by the off-the-record rule had only to find the governors he'd talked with during the day. When they did, the story was there to be written.

There's also the fact that comments from sources who will not be identified can often be written without any source at all. There's no need to quote a source, named or otherwise, on a point of fact that is clearly established. Just state the fact. The Democrats lose an election, and reporters look for an appraisal from party officials. But the party people don't want to be identified because politicians don't like to be identified with defeat.

So they comment on background. One way to write it is the way they put it. " 'We really got beat,' said a Democratic leader, who asked that his name not be used." That's pointless. If they lost the election, they were beaten. Write it that way, flatly; it doesn't need a source.

There is more controversy about sources than understanding. The most thoroughly identified source imaginable is no good if the information is wrong. And the most anonymous of unidentified sources is a treasure if the information is solid.

One night during the Goldwater presidential campaign, two reporters discovered that they could listen to his after-dinner speech in a bar just off the hotel ballroom, taking notes over a drink and watching the proceedings through the doorway. So they did.

A man with a worried look hurried out of the bar in midspeech. He went to the platform and whispered a warning to a Goldwater aide. "Get word to the senator," the man said. "There are two men in the bar writing down every word he says."

In all sourcing, honesty is not only the best policy, it is the mandatory policy. The news comes from sources, open and confidential, and the sources are part of the news. There's as much need for accuracy about sources as for accuracy about the information that makes up a story.

Journalism depends on credibility. If the public doesn't believe what you write, you might as well go into another business. Telling the public where you got the stuff, from government leaks to the coach on the basketball team, is the way to protect that credibility.

We'd all be out of business without it.

8 DELIVERY

GETTING a story is only part of the job, and some days it is the easy part. When you've got nothing to report, the world is full of idle telephones. Let a story break on deadline and there's not an empty pay phone in sight. Pulitzer Prizes have been won because reporters found telephones in the right spot at the right time and told stories as they happened.

Relman Morin of the Associated Press told the story of Little Rock Central High School in 1957 from a telephone booth outside the school, dictating as it unfolded before him:

> At that instant, the eight Negroes—the three boys and five girls— were crossing the schoolyard toward a side door at the south end of the school. The girls were in bobby sox and the boys were dressed in shirts open at the neck.
>
> They were not running, not even walking fast. They simply strolled toward the steps, went up and were inside before all but a few of the 200 people at the end of the street knew it.
>
> "They've gone in," a man roared. "Oh, God, the niggers are in the school."

Morin, who won his second Pulitzer for that story, had a word of advice on dictating breaking copy. "Use the straight, declarative sentence," he said, "subject, verb, predicate. A more complicated sentence can lead you into trouble."

Besides, the stark, uncluttered facts are the most effective way to tell a story like that. Those paragraphs tell the trauma of desegregation more effectively than any essay.

No story counts until it is delivered, or in the trade term, filed. Every reporter faces that imperative every day; indeed, one of the conventions of the trade is that when a colleague has to break away to file while a story is still unfolding, he'll get a recap of what happened when he was gone. It is a code born of self-preservation. Later on, the reporters who protected the absent colleague will have to do their own filing, and he'll cover them for a while.

(There are other tales of reporters covering for reporters. One is of a White House correspondent, suddenly taken drunk while covering Harry S. Truman in Key West, Florida. Sympathetic colleagues figured he'd never be able to file, and three of them decided to help out—without telling each other. All three sent stories back to his paper and signed his name.)

When things are happening, when a story is breaking, it's easy to pick out the reporters whose deadlines are near. They are the ones glancing around every corridor, checking for the telephones. They jingle when they walk, and their pockets wear out regularly. That's because the deadline reporter never goes to work without a pocketful of change. Quarters are best in the era of inflation, since that's enough to get through on any pay telephone.

John Hightower, who won a Pulitzer Prize as an AP diplomatic reporter, found that he could deliver a story more easily by dictating it than by typing it—once he had learned how. "The chief technical problem is advance organization of facts," he said. "The psychological problem is a kind of stage fright, a fear of starting to dictate and then failing to think of the next thing to say."

Once again, it is a matter of practice, of sorting through the facts and seeing the outline of the story before you set about delivering the story. One way to get practice is to look at events that way whether you are covering them or not. In time, it becomes automatic, a reporter's way of thinking.

Such habits pay dividends.

Take March 30, 1981.

When Ronald Reagan was shot outside a Washington hotel, AP reporter Michael Putzel forgot that his tape recorder was running. He had turned it on just in case the President made a comment or two as he boarded a routine motorcade to drive a mile to the White House. Instead, it recorded the five pops of an assassin's pistol, then a moment of stunned silence, then the cries and shouts of bystanders and bodyguards.

It also recorded Putzel's voice, amid the confusion, saying four words. He was talking to himself.

"Get to a phone," he said.

That is the way a professional newsman thinks in a crisis. Get to a telephone. Get there first because news is perishable—and also because within a few minutes, every telephone in dashing distance is going to be taken. Get through to the news desk and deliver the story. And once you've got the line open, hang on to it. You may not get through again, once you hang up.

Or take November 22, 1963.

Jack Bell of the Associated Press and Merriman Smith of United Press International were the wire service reporters riding what is called the White House pool car as President John F. Kennedy rode through Dallas on the way to a speech he never made.

(A White House pool, or any pool, is a delegation of reporters assigned to represent all the rest when—for reasons of space or, all too often, the whim of the president, the candidate or the flack—coverage is limited to a handful of newsmen. The pool reporters, usually representatives of the two major wire services, broadcasters and the daily newspapers, get preferred treatment. They ride near the front of the procession, go to the meetings, hear the speech. The wire service reporters file their own stories, which thus go to every daily newspaper and broadcast outlet. The other pool reporters file reports to their colleagues, so that the entire entourage gets an account of events to which most reporters were not admitted.

(There was a time when the use of pools to represent the traveling press was limited, but the practice has grown in recent years. On some presidential trips nowadays, pool coverage is the rule, general coverage the exception. That means that of two planeloads of reporters who go abroad with a President, perhaps 180 people, only a dozen or so ever see him up close. The rest write their stories from briefings and pool reports.)

In Dallas, Bell was in the back seat of the pool car with two other reporters. Smith was in the front seat, where the mobile telephone was. After rifle fire exploded, Smith grabbed the phone, dialed his bureau and got off the first word.

Here's what it said:

DALLAS, Nov. 22 (UPI)—Three shots were fired at President Kennedy's motorcade today in downtown Dallas.

Later, an add began: "No casualties were reported—"

It was never completed; instead a flash—the designation the wire services reserve for the most extraordinary of events—interrupted.

FLASH:
KENNEDY SERIOUSLY WOUNDED
PERHAPS SERIOUSLY
PERHAPS FATALLY BY ASSASSINS BULLET

All the while, there was a battle for the mobile telephone, Bell demanding his turn, Smith insisting—or pretending—that he hadn't been heard, and continuing to talk to his bureau.

At the instant of the UPI flash, the Associated Press was transmitting a story telephoned in by photographer Ike Altgens, covering the motorcade from the street.

BULLETIN:

DALLAS, Nov. 22 (AP)—President Kennedy was shot today just as his motorcade left downtown Dallas. Mrs. Kennedy jumped up and grabbed Mr. Kennedy. She cried, "Oh, no." The motorcade sped on.

In the pool car of that speeding motorcade, the battle for the telephone continued. Bell finally got it, dialed the Dallas AP bureau, and the phone immediately went dead. No one ever knew why—but Smith was still the man closest to the phone.

Bell jumped from the car as it slowed in the driveway of Parkland Hospital, ran to the President's car and saw Kennedy lying face down on the rear seat. To be doubly certain, he asked a Secret Service agent if it was the President. It was.

He ran into the hospital, found a telephone booth and dictated what he had seen.

(The technology, methods and style of the news business change with changing times. But some aspects do not. Those first sketchy bulletins from Dallas recall the bulletin dispatched by Lawrence A. Gobright on April 14, 1865.

TO THE ASSOCIATED PRESS:

THE PRESIDENT WAS SHOT IN A THEATRE TONIGHT AND PERHAPS MORTALLY WOUNDED.)

Merriman Smith won the Pulitzer Prize for his coverage of the assassination of John F. Kennedy. The first burst of copy he filed over that mobile telephone put his imprint on the story.

Bell, the finest political reporter of his time, never talked much about the episode. He'd done his job that day and done it well, but for want of a phone he was the loser.

Obviously, those are cataclysmic stories, days when a newsman would give whatever kingdom he has to get the facts first, get to a phone and deliver.

There does have to be somebody listening back at the office. Robert MacNeil, then of NBC, tells of jumping from the press bus in Dallas and racing to the first building he saw to find a phone, call New York, and report that shots had been fired at Kennedy. The building turned out to be the Texas School Book Depository. He found a telephone, got his call through—and the deskman in New York, busy with other tasks, said, "Hold on," and put the phone down. Several screams later, MacNeil filed his story.

Most of the time, instant filing is not that crucial. But a newsman never knows when it will be. And the habit of looking for a way to deliver what you have learned is a good habit to develop, whatever the assignment. It's worth a check on the way in, which doesn't take long. You never know when you'll be running on the way out.

The White House press corps landed in Jakarta, Indonesia, a few years ago, covering President Ford. At the hotel, a lot of people wanted to file stories on the telephone, but the Indonesian clerk at the counter said all calls were being delayed by several hours. One reporter changed dollars into rupiahs, the Indonesian currency, and gave the clerk a tip. The reporter got the exchange rate wrong by a very large magnitude, and inadvertently gave the clerk fifty dollars' worth of rupiahs. His call came through in about two minutes; there was no delay at all.

Every reporter has his stock of stories about the trials and traumas of filing copy to meet a deadline that is about to pass. That goes double for reporters who have worked abroad, or under the eye of wartime censors.

Vietnamese censors tried to suppress stories about Buddhist protests during the war there. Under their unwritten rules, the copy wouldn't get out of Saigon. Newsmen found ways around them. The AP bureau in Saigon had a cheesecake photo that was used to test photographic transmission lines. The censors were used to seeing the picture, and didn't pay much attention when it was transmitted. So when things got tough, AP reporters sent the picture of a bathing beauty with a caption reporting the self-immolation of a monk. The censors never looked for the copy there—but the editors in Tokyo did.

Stan Swinton of AP recalled the frustrations of trying to get through balky communications lines and military censorship in Korea. One day he took his copy, put it in a bottle, and threw it into the ocean. A while later, another bottle washed up onto the beach. "My God, I've got a callback already," a competitor said.

In the Middle East, expense-account fortunes have been invested in lining up a telegraph operator or a hotel switchboard to get copy through. There are parts of the world where a story that doesn't get out now may not get out for hours—or days.

When the Shah of Iran staged his international extravaganza on the five thousandth anniversary of the Persian Empire in 1971, leaders from around the world assembled in a luxurious encampment in the desert near Shiraz. And reporters from around the world assembled to cover the show.

The Iranians set up vast press rooms at a university, with row upon row of telex machines to deliver the copy. Since there were more machines than teletype operators, the Iranians trained a corps of college students to punch copy. But most of them spoke only one language: Farsi. They could run the equipment, but they couldn't comprehend the copy. Within a day or so, most savvy reporters were punching their own copy into the machines, while the operators watched.

One less-than-savvy reporter, covering Vice-President Agnew, dutifully filed his stories to the AP bureau in Teheran, for relay to London and on to New York. It went nowhere, because the AP man stationed in Teheran was in Shiraz himself. So an office assistant in Teheran filed it all back to Shiraz. It finally got out a day late, but nobody seemed to care. Agnew wasn't making much news in those days.

Then, too, there are the agonies of a reporter trying to dictate to a rewrite man who is hard of hearing, or to a dictationist who doesn't speak much English. It happens.

One night in Los Angeles, a political reporter set about filing a piece on a speech by then presidential nominee Barry Goldwater. He called the desk. (In the news business, a desk is not just a piece of furniture. It is also the people who take copy, edit it and put it in the paper, on the wire or on the air. They sit at desks and they are The Desk. Omnipotent, but sometimes a bit deaf.)

The reporter called in, dictated the dateline and the lead paragraph, then came to a sentence including the words: "Goldwater said that . . ." The process had taken a good ten minutes by then, and that was before "that." The exchange from that point went this way:

Reporter: Goldwater said that—
Desk: What's that?
Reporter: Goldwater said that—
Desk: Say that again.
Reporter: Said that—
Desk: I didn't get that.
Reporter: That.
Desk: How's that?
Reporter: Forget it.

That is one story that never got filed. The world is probably no poorer for that.

But the trouble is not always at the receiving end of the phone line. Too often, the reporter tries to dictate a story without organizing it in his own mind. All of us are accustomed to composing at the typewriter or the video terminal. It always helps to see it in writing. But there are going to be times when that is not possible. Then is when the newsman needs to know how to dictate from notes or ad-lib on the air.

In some jobs it won't happen often. In some, it is essential, and becomes routine. There are still operations that do it the old-fashioned way: The reporter collects information, telephones his desk and blurts it all out. A rewrite man puts it into English.

But there are a lot more in which the reporter is the writer too, whether at the typewriter or in a telephone booth across town.

The knack of organizing a story without seeing it on paper is one that serves well when time and circumstances do permit the reporter to write at the typewriter. If you could have dictated it from notes, then the structure of the story, the order in which it should be told, and many of the words with which to tell it are already set in your mind. With that settled, you can spend more effort on the writing itself. The mechanical part is out of the way, and you can lend the story some style.

Story organization away from the typewriter is essential in many broadcast situations, for a reporter must be able to go on the air live and describe something that has just happened.

The best way to do it is not to be overwhelmed by notes, but to use them to make a brief outline of what's to be said. The whole story needn't be outlined, but the lead and the closing line should be settled. With practice, the rest will take care of itself. A few minutes spent preparing an outline can make an ad-libbed report a very well organized piece of work. And the more you do it, the fewer minutes it takes.

The class of the league, any league, as a newswriting stylist was Associated Press reporter Doug Cornell, who covered the White House for a generation, and wrote every major Washington story of his time. His work was distinctive to the point that a Cornell story was identifiable whether it carried his by-line or not. And his best work was done off the cuff.

After all those years at the White House, filing from notes on stories that would not wait to be written, Cornell could dictate flawless copy. It was fast, it was smooth, and it was done without benefit of the typewriter. "Speaker of the House Sam Rayburn, a small man of great national stature, died today in the little Texas town he loved," Cornell dictated from Bonham, Texas, in 1961.

He reached a point at which the typewriter got in the way. One night Cornell was assigned to put together a story rounding up assorted primary elections around the country. Returns rolled in, but the story didn't roll out. He sat at the typewriter, struggling.

Finally, a new staffer went over and asked if he could help. "Yes," Cornell said, a bit embarrassed. "Could you sit over there and let me call you?" And he motioned to a desk on the other side of the room.

That's how it was done. The new man went to the far desk, the veteran called him up and, from a pile of election returns, notes and comments, dictated the story, fast and clean.

The typewriter, the telephone, the video display terminal and, for that matter, the pencil and notebook or the tape recorder all are tools, and the people who do newswriting best use them as second nature, automatically. That way they don't intrude on the product, which, after all, is only one thing: the story that goes into the paper or onto the air.

A reporter who can use any or all of those tools without thinking about it a whole lot is going to have a decided advantage over one who needs to stop and consider each step in delivery.

Some newspeople take shorthand; more develop their own personal shorthand and take notes in a personal code no one else could decipher. Even shorthand can get in the way. Years ago at a trial in Boston, a reporter who knew shorthand took stenographic notes, and then had to ask colleagues to go over their longhand notes with him so he could find the really significant quotes and put together a story. Having too much in your notebook can be as severe a problem as having too little. The whole process is one of selectivity, and the selecting has to begin at the beginning of the story. So the best reporters don't write down every word. They only write down the important ones. The best reporters know which ones those are. That sounds more mysterious than it is. If it strikes you as significant, new, different, colorful, or just interesting, write it down and put it into the story. If it doesn't, go on to the next element of the event you are covering, and apply the same test. You'll make mistakes in that winnowing process, and there will be editors to tell you so. But you will be right more often than not.

And when it comes time to file, you'll have a handle on the story that will make it easier to deliver the copy on time and in shape.

Some stories are embargoed, which leads to quirks in the delivery of copy. An embargo is a release time, a story based on material that was available in advance of the hour or day of publication. The simplest example is the text of a speech. A President is going to address a joint session of Congress at 8 P.M. The White House Press Office distributes a text in advance, say at 5 P.M. The story is written and ready when the speech begins.

Lengthy government reports are handled that way, which is sensible, since a newsman confronted with a thousand pages of text is not going to be able to do it justice without some time to read it. There are exceptions, and they make life difficult. For example, the Supreme Court never issues its decisions before they are read from the bench. On a major case, the opinion and dissents can run to hundreds of pages. They are pages of intricate judicial reasoning, and the authors have spent days, even weeks, in drafting them. The reporters who handle the copy have a few minutes to figure them out and file stories on what the court has decided. Under the circumstances, the miracle is that the stories are almost always right.

Embargoed copy is routine. Most news releases—"handouts" is the trade term—are headed with the embargo time. The Sunday papers are a favorite release target for politicians and public relations men. When there is a story in one of those handouts, it is withheld from publication until 6:30 P.M. Saturday. When the embargoed material is for an afternoon newspaper, it is not for publication until 6:30 A.M. on the release date. Those are the flat release times for AMs—morning papers— and PMs—those published in the afternoon. A great deal of material is put out in advance for release on delivery, at a 10 A.M. congressional hearing, or an evening political rally.

There also are embargoes timed to go with a presidential announcement or, in matters diplomatic, a simultaneous release in other capitals. Occasionally, reporters embargo their own material. A group of newsmen interview a public figure, for example, and decide to wait a day before publishing the story, not for any sinister reason but because they want time to get background, check other sources and write at leisure.

Embargoes can lead to hassles. In advance of a major presidential announcement on strategic weapons, the Pentagon held an embargoed briefing to discuss details of the proposal. At the same time, Pentagon emissaries were describing the plan to selected members of Congress. In Washington, advance briefings are a form of flattery and a head start on lobbying. What members of Congress hear, members of Congress usually tell. A reporter put together details of the weapons proposal by talking to congressmen, wrote the story, put it in the paper, and promptly was accused by outraged Pentagon flacks of breaking their embargo.

Don't worry about situations like that. The flacks need you more than you need them. Go by the rules, but write what you've learned. Once you've accepted an embargo, you're bound by it. There is no code of conduct for reporters, but if there were, that would be in it.

MEARS: I got into an embargo flap one night on the island of Crete. I was covering Agnew, one of a half-dozen reporters on the trip. We interviewed him on the airplane flying into Crete. I checked into the hotel, and started transcribing my notes. I'd done that and was working on a story on the interview, when I got a phone call from an Agnew aide, who said he was meeting with the other reporters to talk about a transcript of the interview. I'd made my own, so I told him that whatever they decided about the transcript was all right with me. What they decided was to wait overnight for it, until the secretaries traveling with Agnew had typed it out. In essence, they decided to embargo the story.

The upshot was that I wound up violating an embargo I didn't know existed. I filed the story back to New York and a summary line moved on the wire for afternoon papers. The other reporters promptly got callbacks and just as promptly accused me of doing them dirt by breaking the embargo. I hadn't agreed to it, but I'd skipped the meeting and felt obligated to observe it. So I called my New York desk, they withdrew the summary line and held the story off the wire until the release time later that day. They thought I'd gone crazy. I thought I had, too, since I'd spent half the night working on the story when I could have been sampling the pleasures of Crete.

By the time I got it straightened out, I was angry at myself, the world, and the other five reporters. Especially the other five reporters. They kept complaining about the episode as we set out to cover Agnew on a tour of the island. Finally, one of them accused me of breaking the embargo because that was the only way I could beat him. (The word "scoop" is used in movies. What it really is is a beat.) He ventured this opinion as we approached the court of King Minos. I observed gently that I could beat him on any story on the worst day I ever had, underscoring this observation with four-letter emphasis. He kept at it and I decided that he had better be punched in the face. Since he was standing beside the labyrinth at the time, the punch I had in mind would have knocked him into the lair of the Minotaur, who, unfortunately, was no longer there.

All of this was in the final planning stage when Agnew and his security phalanx walked upon the scene, so it never happened. That's just as well, since the jails in Crete probably are not very pleasant. But I think there was immortality, of a sort, to be had as the reporter who belted another reporter into the labyrinth over a story release time.

CHANCELLOR: It's nice to have company, but staying with a crowd of reporters is not always a good idea. Back in the fifties, I found myself in Jordan. There had been a small rebellion against King Hussein, and the British Army had moved in troops to occupy the airport near Amman. There were a lot of reporters there, mainly British. One day the British ambassador threw a party for the visiting press, but two of us were not invited, the man from the *Christian Science Monitor* and me. I guess we weren't on his list. So we sat cooling our heels in the hotel lobby as everyone else went off to the embassy. I said, "Let's go and see the king." My friend from the *Monitor* said we would never be admitted to the palace, but I thought we ought to try. We went there, said we knew our visit was unorthodox, but we were in town and thought we'd like to pay our respects to His Majesty. And by God, he appeared in about ten minutes, gave us some tea and some news. There were a lot of callbacks the next day and some grumbling on the part of our colleagues. But we had shown again the value of asking for something. Always ask, *always.* They can only say no, and they often surprise you by saying yes. It's basic.

Embargoed copy, a routine part of the business, can create practical and ethical problems. It did for Edward Kennedy, an AP war correspondent during World War II. Kennedy was in a pool of newsmen who went to the brick schoolhouse in Reims,

France, on May 7, 1945, to witness the unconditional surrender of Nazi Germany. What they saw and learned was embargoed, pending official release the following day. But between the time of the surrender and the time of the embargo, the war actually ended. The shooting stopped. The word was out all over Paris. A German radio station, under Allied supervision, broadcast news of the surrender to the troops. Allied troops were informed. The American Office of War Information broadcast the surrender story in Paris.

Harry S. Truman and Winston Churchill had acceded to a Soviet request that nothing be made public pending a formal surrender ceremony in Berlin. That was going to take time.

So Kennedy broke the embargo. He filed his story from Paris to London, using an army telephone. It cleared two censorship barriers, and was sent on to AP in New York. The war was over.

It was a costly beat.

The censors clamped down in Paris. Other correspondents were not allowed to file what they, like Kennedy, knew. Fifty-four of them signed a protest against what they called "the most disgraceful, deliberate and unethical double cross in the history of journalism." Kennedy was summoned back to New York, and within a year, he was out of AP.

He had the story, he knew how to deliver it, and he felt that it should not be withheld from people who believed their men still faced the peril of a war that was over. The men who were not fighting anymore knew it; the people at home did not until he filed. But that left, and leaves, the troublesome question of a newsman's obligation to other reporters who have the same information—and the same instincts.

The controversy overshadowed the way Kennedy wrote the story. He did it simply and plainly—and with one minor but irritating error, penciled in by an editor who thought he knew better than the reporter. Kennedy began this way:

REIMS, France, May 7 (AP)—Germany surrendered uncondi-
tionally to the Western Allies and the Soviet Union at 2:41 A.M.
French time today.

The surrender took place at a little red schoolhouse that is the
headquarters of General Dwight D. Eisenhower.

Kennedy had described the place as a big red schoolhouse,
which it was. The adjective was changed at a copy desk far from
Reims, and as a result, a sprawling high school that covered
most of a city block will forever be remembered as the little red
schoolhouse where Germany surrendered.

A. J. Liebling, a fine war correspondent himself, said he
suspected that what made the other newsmen so angry was that
they forgot about the telephone line Kennedy remembered and
used to deliver the story.

CHANCELLOR: The government of Lebanon established
    censorship on news reports during the civil war in
    1958. There were a lot of American correspondents
    there because the U.S. Marines had landed in Lebanon,
    and all of us were struggling with the censors. We
    learned that the officers who censored newspaper copy
    were far more thorough than the ones who censored
    radio copy. I told this to the late William Lawrence,
    then of the New York *Times,* later of ABC News. A
    day or two later, he came to me with a proposal. The
    Times owns a radio station in New York, WQXR.
    Would I be good enough to get Mr. Lawrence
    accredited as a radio correspondent for WQXR? I
    introduced him to the right people, and the next day he
    began reading his dispatches to the *Times* into a
    microphone, on a line headed for WQXR. It was
    transcribed there, sent to the *Times*'s foreign desk, and
    from then on he was often a full day ahead of his
    competition.

The instinct is always the same: to get the story and to tell it. That can lead to mistakes.

The old United Press (it's called the old as opposed to the new, three-initial UPI, born in 1958 with the takeover of International News Service, which used to be the third U.S. wire service) ended World War I prematurely with an armistice bulletin on November 7, 1918. There were celebrations in the streets, and threats of violence against AP offices for not reporting the same thing. The armistice came on November 11.

No service and no newsman is immune from the pitfalls a pressure business can create.

An AP editor set up an elaborate system of radio relays from the courtroom to an attic transmitter in order to get first word of the verdict in the trial of Bruno Hauptmann, convicted in 1935 of kidnapping the Lindbergh baby. The word came through as planned—the verdict was no. 4. The message was repeated. Four was the code for conviction, and life imprisonment. That was wrong, and nobody ever figured out what had happened. In the effort at instant delivery, the AP man outsmarted the system of courtroom security—and outsmarted himself. The story of the verdict—the wrong verdict—moved on AP wires before the jury returned. When it did return, the verdict was guilty; the penalty, death. AP reporters in the courtroom wrote it out, messengers delivered it to the editor, and it moved within one minute of the jury foreman's announcement.

Codes have been used to get important stories past governments' restrictions. For example, it was once the practice of the government of Italy to stop all cable traffic, news and commercial, when a pope died, in order to let the Vatican time its own announcement. When one pope died, the announcement was held up for twenty hours.

So in 1914, the UP bureau manager in Rome arranged a code to tell his New York headquarters of the death of Pius X, and the code scored a nine-hour beat for UP over AP.

UP used a code again in 1922 when Benedict XV was on his deathbed. The code for the death was a message reading "SEND TRUNKS IMMEDIATELY." But one Saturday morning, before the wires had opened, UP New York staffers came to work to find cables (sent through various cities to guarantee that they would arrive) reading both "SEND TRUNKS IMMEDIATELY" and "UNSEND TRUNKS IMMEDIATELY." It was hard to tell which one to believe and they couldn't get through to Rome on the telephone. UP decided on caution and did not announce the death of the Pope.

It was a bad day for UP. AP said he was dead, and there were angry calls from UP clients. In the end, as is so often the case, caution turned out to be the right course. The Pope didn't die until the next day. "UNSEND TRUNKS IMMEDIATELY" was the right message.

It is possible to try too hard to deliver too fast. News won't wait for long, but it can wait a minute. The first words you hear are not necessarily the story.

When Ronald Reagan bawled out his budget director, David A. Stockman, for saying in interviews that he doubted the administration's economic program would work, there was a predictable offer of resignation. Stockman then held a news conference, and said near the start of it that he had tendered his resignation.

BULLETIN:
WASHINGTON (UPI)—Budget Director David Stockman, under fire for remarks critical of President Reagan's economic policies, said Thursday he is resigning.

But the writer hadn't waited long enough to get the full story. President Reagan had not accepted the resignation. A second bulletin got the story straight. Sometimes it pays to wait a bit.

The people you're covering, and the imagemakers who work for them, try to reason out ways to get what they want printed into the paper. Sometimes politicians crack the code of the news business, and use it to good advantage.

Joe McCarthy made superb use of the media. In those days, the 35 mm cameras used for television news were bulky, and it was almost impossible for them to film every word of one of his speeches. McCarthy would go to the television reporters and cameramen and tell them he would bang his fist on the side of the lectern when he got to what he called the "fresh news" in his speech. The networks filmed what they thought was news, but when the fist banged on the lectern, *all* the cameras were sure to be on.

Senator William Proxmire, who represents the same state but an entirely different set of political precepts, often issued his press releases for publication in Monday newspapers. That's good timing for maximum exposure, because not much happens on Sundays and a story available for Monday publication is likely to get good display. Proxmire has been known to hold committee hearings in the middle of a congressional recess. No other senators would show up, but reporters would. During a congressional session, a routine hearing probably would draw a couple of reporters with notebooks, and none with television crews. When there is no other show in town, it can draw a crowd and make the network news.

To repeat: Keep an eye open for telephones. Should your career take you to more exotic locales, follow the foreign correspondent's first rule and when you get to town, check to see how and when you can get copy out of town.

Telephones, by the way, can cost a lot more than a quarter. When there is a story breaking, it is worth ten, twenty or even fifty dollars to get the shopkeeper across the street to hold his line open for you. There is no honor among newsmen when it comes to grabbing the telephone, so make the bid enough to buy the shopkeeper's loyalty for a while. Otherwise you can dash back to the store to find a new customer on the phone, at a better rate.

When there is a continuing story far from communications, it is worth the investment to have a special line installed. When Reagan was putting his administration together and the briefings were held outside his California home, AP rented a tree from a neighbor and had a phone installed on it. The rent was fifty dollars, not including the phone. About the time it was all set up, Reagan moved his base of operations.

Newsmen have been known to unscrew the mouthpiece of a pay phone, take out the gismo that makes it work, and leave the phone out of order—until they come back, put it together again, and use it. Telephone repairmen carry stickers that read "Out of Order." Some reporters do too. If the other guy thinks the phone doesn't work, he may leave it open until you need it.

A bit of guile doesn't hurt in getting a story and in getting it out.

Overseas, the traveling reporter sometimes must file by cable, and it isn't inexpensive. You'll find editors particularly devoted to brevity when it costs a dime a word to get the stuff into the office. That's why foreign correspondents sometimes write in cablese, which has its own set of perils. All the words that get omitted to save tolls are words that add clarity, and without them a sentence can be misinterpreted.

Witness the story of the small Colorado paper, the Walsenburg *World-Independent,* that wanted a special report on the outcome of the 1933 Indianapolis 500 automobile race. The editor wired the AP bureau in Indianapolis to ask for a telegram on the outcome of the race, since the finish would come after his regular wire service had ended for the day. A message like that is called an overhead.

Later that day, the AP wired back a confirming message: "WILL OVERHEAD WINNER 500." The editor had all he needed for a story telling how Will Overhead had won the race in an upset, his victory all the more startling because he was such a long shot that he hadn't even been listed in the entries.

Cables from headquarters can be nasty, even when that isn't

the intent. Take the young reporter assigned to cover the Guantánamo Bay Naval Base during the Cuban missile crisis of 1962. There wasn't much going on at Guantánamo, but it was the closest an American reporter could get to the scene of the crisis.

So the reporter cranked out copy—features, interviews, mood pieces. And hustled it to the All America Cables office, where it was dispatched to New York at a nickel a word.

Back came a message from the desk: "COPY MAGNIFICENT. KEEP IT COMING. PLEASE MAIL FUTURELY." That's cablese meaning from now on send it for the price of a postage stamp instead.

Were the White House to announce that President Reagan was planning a quick trip to Paris someday this week, accompanied by his wife, it could be translated into cablese as "REAGAN PARISWARD SWEEK CUMNANCY."

Cablese is a dying language, because filing copy by cable is slow and expensive. Telephones, telex and high-speed transmission lines are cheaper and more efficient.

"Delivery" has more than one meaning for broadcast journalists. One of its meanings is the way broadcasters speak on the air. There are no immutable rules. Chances are, a news organization won't let someone on the air with a serious speech defect, or a voice pitched so high or so low as to make it stand out. That kind of thing gets in the way of delivery.

Great pipes do not a journalist make. Orson Welles and Richard Burton and others in the theater have marvelous voices, but they might not be credible newspeople because they sound so out of the ordinary.

The secret of successful broadcast delivery is that there is no secret. The most effective broadcasters are those who sound on the air the way they sound in person. If they speak well in their personal lives, chances are they'll succeed on the air.

CHANCELLOR: For years, I had a nervous cough which
    drove me crazy. I tried everything to soothe my throat
    —honey in hot tea, all the rest of the cures—and

nothing worked. I still was stuck with one of the most widely amplified postnasal drips in history. Finally, I went to a throat doctor, and he told me to take a mild tranquilizer an hour before each broadcast. All it did was calm me down, and I stopped coughing. The trouble hadn't been in my throat. It had been in my head. Eventually I stopped the tranquilizer, and the coughing never came back.

Aside from medication, which is complicated, or alcohol, which is ruinous, the best cure for nervousness is experience. No one is going to be perfect that first time on the air, but after a while, most people calm down and just do their work.

Calmness is a key quality for a broadcaster. There have been some notable shouters in the business, and there are a few around today, but if an audience is to tune in and listen to the news over a period of years, the shouting can get awfully grating.

There are ways of emphasizing, of verbally underlining, certain facts. Whenever David Brinkley gets to a particularly important or surprising fact, he repeats it. "It's the first time that has happened in fifty years, fifty years," he will say. He doesn't raise his voice. The repetition does the job.

The pause is useful—a hesitation before the important quote or the staggering statistic. It sends a signal to the audience that something important is about to be said. "The government reported today that the national debt has reached"—tiny pause—"a trillion dollars." But pausers should beware: if it lasts longer than one second, it gets hammy very quickly.

Sometimes emphasis can be achieved through characterization. If something is out of the ordinary, use a word or two to describe it that way. "The mayor, who is always reluctant to comment on city council decisions, did say . . ." If you think something is relevant in a story, find a way to say so without raising your voice.

There are some broadcast journalists who hate to ad-lib.

They want their words written down before they're spoken, because they're afraid they'll get lost, or make a mistake if they are asked an unexpected question. These people lead hard lives, and it's a shame, because ad-libbing is as easy as, well, talking.

Jack Paar, a talk-show host of some years ago, once observed that ad-libbing wasn't difficult; he pointed out that we all do it all the time, which is true. But broadcasters add something: They have a clear idea of what they want to say. It may be a scribbled word or two, a single word setting forth an idea. Sometimes it is held in reserve. But when things get uncomfortable, the broadcaster reaches into his mental file for something he has thought out beforehand.

There is a lot of ad-libbing on local television news programs. The smart reporter who has covered the fire, the speech or the auction saves up a piece of color or a good quote from the story, and when prompted by the anchorpeople, pulls out that information and uses it, off the cuff. It is ad-libbed, but the reporter was prepared to use it. A professional always has something ready.

Floor reporters covering national political conventions for the networks use this technique. The reason they never seem at a loss for words is that they keep a file in their heads, a catalogue of things they've seen on the convention floor so they'll have something to say when called upon.

A second meaning of the word "delivery," for anchorpeople, is delivery of the goods—of information. At a political convention, or on an election night, or at a space shot or in a crisis, everything is ad-libbed. Information is delivered for hours, as it happens. Much of it is hard news and a lot of it is analysis.

Did Kentucky go Republican? If it did, that's news, but it is often equally important to say how Kentucky has gone in the past. Did Nixon carry it in the 1968 squeaker? How did this border state react to the candidate from Georgia, who won in 1976?

The same blend of news and background applies to on-the-air

coverage at the state or local level. The local anchorpeople have to supply perspective and analysis, and they have to do it while the story is breaking, because that is when the audience needs it. There's no time to write.

The organization of this background material is critical to the success of the broadcast—and the broadcaster. Floundering around is bad for one's professional health. An anchorperson must always have something to say, something relevant and informative if the job is to be done well.

The key is the broadcaster's command of that material. The hard news is easy: It is either directly observed, as in a hold in a spaceship's countdown, or a vote on a convention floor, or it comes in written down on a piece of wire copy. Reporting that is the easy part.

The tough part is what do you say next? And that's where the organization of background material becomes paramount.

CHANCELLOR: Different people organize their information in different ways. Brinkley and Tom Brokaw use small, indexed loose-leaf notebooks. When they read or hear something pertinent, sometimes months before the event, they write it down. It's there when they need it. My technique involves charts, which I make out on large cards, cut to fit on the anchor desk.

For example, in covering presidential elections, I use one fairly large chart divided into 51 sections—all the states and the District of Columbia. And into each section I put a lot of information in color-coded shorthand. Republican statistics are blue, Democrat red. Economic data, like state unemployment statistics, are in black. Political folklore about the state is in green. And so on. When the chart is done, it has on it more than a thousand separate facts, all there on a card about a foot and a half deep by two feet wide. This is actually less work than it seems, and when you put the figures down yourself, they get into your head. It is hard to work quickly with research done by others. I make up smaller charts with national information, poll closing times, national registration and turnout figures, things like that. When we go on the air election nights, I've got maybe half a dozen large and small charts.

It is a faster information-retrieval system than a computer. In less than a second, I can look down, find my state figures, and ad-lib endlessly: the history of past elections; is the state rich or poor in terms of per capita income; the balance between city people and country people; the size of minority groups. It's handy to have this stuff right there in front of you when things get dull, or when the computers suddenly go out to lunch, which happens once in a while.

I use charts on just about all predictable special events. When someone like President Sadat gets shot, you have to wing it, but I keep clipping files in the office, and I usually grab what I've saved, even if the news story has just broken and I'm on my way to the studio.

Preparation is everything in live, on-the-air reporting assignments that can be planned in advance. Four or five hours of preparation for every hour on the air is not unusual for network anchors. During the week of a national convention, they may be on the air as much as forty-eight hours in three or four days. The preparation that goes into those forty-eight hours is immense, but if it's done right, the audience never knows it. And that's the way it should be.

MEARS: There isn't any one right way to prepare for a story. You've got to go in knowing what you're talking about. My way of preparing is to write it out. If I'm going to be writing the story of a national election, I go over the background and the latest campaign information state by state and type out notes to myself, some on index cards and some on plain copy paper. I'll wind up with a sheaf of notes—names, numbers, what happened last election, and so on. I put them all in order and then go to work. And usually find that by the time I could use all those details, the current information is piling up so fast that it is all I can handle. The most useful background is what I've crammed into my head, and I get it there by the process of typing out all those notes.

A final word on delivering stories:

Most journalists seldom encounter the kind of pressures that go with reporting for a wire service, or reporting on the air without a script.

There usually is ample time before deadline. Once in a while a story breaks just before the paper goes to press or the broadcast begins. But that is the exception.

But time is a deceptive luxury.

In a sort of journalistic application of Parkinson's Law, reporting and writing expand to fill the available time until deadline. Don't let them. When you've got the story in hand, write it as though it had to be done right now. It will be a better story. Everything that will go into it is not in your notebook; some of it is in your head, in impressions and observations that will fade quickly. You can always go back for more reporting, or rewrite and polish what you've done. But that first story usually will be the best, and what you do later will be fine tuning.

Tell it right now and you'll tell it the way you saw it. Put it off and that will become more difficult. Not to mention the fact that you might miss dinner.

9 *HOW TO GET STARTED*

THE quandary is that you can't get a job in journalism unless you've got experience and you can't get experience unless you have a job.

The puzzle that poses is not insoluble, but getting it solved isn't easy. It takes determination, commitment, endurance, imagination and some luck. The more luck the better.

The best luck is to have a family that owns a newspaper or a television station, but since that solution is not generally available, it is better to stipulate that heirs and heiresses quit reading this and go to work.

For the rest of us, a starting point toward starting work is to concentrate on the first problem and work on experience. You can make your own experience by practice, by establishing the habits and disciplines of a reporter.

"Give the same set of facts to a room full of reporters and each will arrange the facts in a slightly different way," wrote Don Whitehead, who covered war and government for the Associated Press. "This is not important if the end results are accurate. . . . The important differences in them will be the degree of skill used in making the story interesting.

"This skill is achieved only through experience in writing. There are no shortcuts."

There's the word again. Experience.

There was a time not long ago when editors—or, more often, publishers—took advantage of the quest for experience with magnanimous offers of jobs at no pay. Beginners would get paid in experience. That's rare now, although there is a modern variation in what are called internships, jobs at little or no pay that become part of a journalism student's college education.

With or without a job or an internship, the most important kind of experience is easily available. It is practice, experience gained by viewing events and writing about them. It is the only way to learn; a teacher or a book can guide you, but no one else can provide the experience of writing. So look around and write about it. Publish it if you can, save it if you can't. Either way, it is experience. It's better if somebody pays you to do it, but if they won't, do it anyway.

The editor who holds the key to that first job may—probably will—say that he'd like it better if you had come to him with a couple of years as a professional journalist on your résumé. It makes his job easier; you're a proven performer and won't need as much care and feeding as a recruit.

But if you can sit down at the typewriter and put together a story like the professional you're not, that attitude can be altered in a hurry. The editor with a job opening will find such competence a lot more compelling than a sheaf of clippings that carry your by-line. Everybody who wants in has a sheaf of clippings, but your name at the top does not necessarily mean that you wrote the polished copy underneath. The editor knows that better than anyone else; he's been rewriting—or ghostwriting—copy for years.

It is reasonable to expect that you will get a salary, although not a very handsome one, while gaining professional experience by doing a job. It is not reasonable to expect that somebody will pay you to practice in order to learn how to do that job. That part is up to you.

There are as many ways into the news business as there are journalists, but all of them have one thing in common: persistence. It isn't a calling people drift into just to have a job. The pay isn't good enough for that, the hours are lousy and the competition is intense. The people who do it really want to do it.

H. L. Mencken, one of the most influential journalists in American history, stood for thirty-seven nights in the corner of the city room of the Baltimore *Morning Herald,* waiting for an unpaid assignment. For the next six months he worked all day for his family's tobacco business and nearly all night for the *Herald,* until the paper hired him as a reporter.

Starting early helps. A. M. Rosenthal, now executive editor of the New York *Times,* began as a part-time campus correspondent for the paper and has never worked anywhere else. He was in his teens when he began.

CHANCELLOR: I managed to land a job as a copy boy on the old Chicago *Times* (later to become the *Sun-Times*) and rose to the position of city desk assistant, which meant I answered the phones. For about six months, I would work the four-to-twelve shift on the city desk, and then ride with the midnight-shift photographers until eight in the morning. I think I really got my job because the photographers were willing to help me, to let me write their captions. The Newspaper Guild could have beefed about my working the extra shift for no pay, but nobody complained, and after half a year of sixteen-hour days I was signed on as a full-time reporter.

MEARS: I never wanted to do anything else and when I got to college, I headed for the campus newspaper. I spent more time there than in class, and dealt on some stories with the college public relations man, who knew an AP man, who got me an interview with the Boston bureau chief, who gave me a summer relief job at $55 a week in 1955. I went back after I graduated—by then the pay was up to $60—and stayed.

David Halberstam worked on the *Harvard Crimson* during his undergraduate days. He met a Southern newspaperman who was doing graduate work on a fellowship and who helped him to land a beginner's job on a small Southern daily. For beginners, friends in the business can be vital.

Some come in close to the top. George Will, impelled by a love for conservative politics and possessed of a considerable skill with words, went from a senator's office to become the Washington essayist for *The National Review* and then to national syndication as a columnist.

Egbert Roscoe Murrow, who changed his name to Edward while in college, got into broadcast journalism without any previous news experience. CBS hired him as its director of talks in 1935. He lied about his age because he thought he was too young for the job. He was twenty-seven at the time.

Murrow was a producer, but one day, with the help of a few drinks, he forced himself onto the air. It was, perhaps, the most unusual debut in the history of the business.

Here is how Alexander Kendrick, Murrow's friend and biographer, tells it:

There had been a Christmas party in the CBS newsroom, and when the time came for [Bob] Trout's evening news program, Murrow took over the microphone instead and wrestled the script from him, with the explanation that Trout had enjoyed the party too well. He began reading the news.

Trout, a temperate man in every sense of the word, realized that Murrow was the one who had overindulged and waited for evidence of it, in the form of slurred words and fumbling phrases. But Murrow never faltered. He marched through the news clearly and precisely, as if it had been made for him, and he for it.

Luckily for Murrow, and for the profession, that worked. It is not a good idea.

Murrow was a natural. He had instinctive story sense, a feeling for history and an uncommon talent as a writer. Every generation produces a few naturals, people with the right combinations of personality, skill and determination.

They share one trait: they all work very hard at what they do. It is almost impossible to coast into journalism. That may have something to do with one of the truths about the craft itself: there are lucky reporters, but there never are lazy lucky reporters. The willingness to work hard is essential.

The people who figure it all out the first day are rare exceptions. Most beginners are not that way, but are, rather, people with talent and ambition who need time to develop those attributes into the skills of a journalist.

Some of them are drawn by what seems to be the romance of the trade, a press card for that hatband and some walking-around money for the assignment to San Francisco or Paris that surely will be coming soon. They don't last. It doesn't take long for realism to catch up with the notion that there's another Watergate out there, waiting for the right reporter to win honors and riches at an early age.

Better to look at the realities of newspaper life as you go in, and here are some of them:

—There are more applicants than openings, year after year, and the jobs that are open don't pay very well. College graduates who go into journalism make less money than their classmates, sometimes a lot less. That is most pronounced at the starting level, but it is true—with few exceptions—at every stage of a reporter's career.

In 1980, journalism schools graduated 14,600 people. Fewer

than 3,000 of them went to work for newspapers. For those who did, the average starting wage was $9,900 a year. The government figured that a family with an income of $8,414 or less that year was living in poverty.

—The hours are awful. There's a lot of drudgery, late at night. There are overnight shifts to be filled, midnight to morning, and as soon as you learn what you're doing, you'll probably have to take your turn on one like that. Plan on sleeping days. Don't count on weekends and don't count on holidays. The news goes on, and it has to be covered, even if it does mean working on Christmas Eve.

—You'll have to be nosy in a way most people would consider offensive. You'll have to ask unpleasant questions, sometimes in difficult circumstances. Nobody likes to intrude on a grieving family, but death, and therefore grief, are part of the news.

Journalism is a more secure profession today than it was a few decades ago, when capricious editors could fire at will. There is more stability because it is in the interests of managers, and because union contracts guarantee job security. The pay is better than it used to be, for the same reasons.

The work has become more specialized, and news organizations have an incentive to pay more in order to keep their people. The era of the vagabond newsman is long past. The classified advertisements no longer warn that no drinkers need apply. Would-be employers do not make that assumption about newspeople, which is not to say they don't drink, some to excess.

Journalism is a profession in the sense that it requires special talents and training. Most modern journalists are college people, middle-class people. The press club bar is not what it used to be. Most of the members spend cocktail hour commuting to the suburbs.

Salaries may not be great, but they aren't bad. A reporter

who gains journeyman status, which means five or six years in the business, will, in most major cities, earn a contract minimum of $30,000 or more. That was the level in the early 1980s, and while it wasn't wealth, it was a living. And the best do better, some of them much better.

Still, journalism doesn't offer the safeguards of the law, medicine, engineering or accounting. It is part artistry and part routine. A newspaper has to be assembled, just like an automobile. The job may be guaranteed, but there is no assurance that a veteran who runs afoul of the editor for one reason or another won't find himself doing drudge work on the late-night trick.

Editors come and go, news companies fail, technology changes, new owners arrive, and the competition for positions and promotions always is tough. It is a risky business.

Those who survive and progress are those with drive, determination and the natural talents of journalists. There are also a good many bitter, even broken, middle-aged people in the news business, survivors putting in their time.

Enough of the perils and drawbacks. Done well, for an employer who values a job done well, it is a beguiling and endlessly interesting life. It also is useful; it produces something of particular value to the community and the nation. And it's fun.

It is not a life that must be lived in Washington or New York, London or Peking. There are stories to cover and much to be accomplished in any community. And there are a lot of happy and successful people who prefer small-town journalism. One of the rewards is to see the impact of one's work, and it shows more clearly at the local than at the national or international level.

The way to begin is not at the top. The Washington bureau is where you get, not where you start.

The work a reporter does in Washington or for a television network is not markedly different from that at a state capitol or a local TV station. Politicians are politicians, whether they be mayors or Presidents, city council members or congressmen.

The stage is smaller at city hall or the statehouse. But the audience often is far more attentive. That's true also for the man or woman anchoring a local news program. There is an interplay with the readers and viewers that seldom happens at the national level.

More and more young Americans get their start in journalism classes. In 1981, more than 77,000 students were majoring in journalism. Many use school placement departments to help them land a first job. Schools of journalism are useful not only for what they teach, but because they can help bright beginners to get started. Most schools have professional journalists on the faculty, and they can be a big help, for what they know and for who they know.

For the young man or woman seeking a way into the news business, all the numbers are not depressing. Not with 1,730 daily newspapers and 7,666 weeklies in the United States in 1981. Among the dailies, 1,353 published in the afternoon. Thirty more were "all day" papers, with editions morning and night.

So the odds are that your most promising job target is a small or middle-sized afternoon daily newspaper, simply because there are more of them. There are jobs there.

There are more jobs on the weeklies, and on the more than 8,900 radio stations and the 1,000-plus television stations in the United States.

The question is where. The answer probably is closer than you think. There are too many would-be journalists who think they're getting into some kind of show business and want to go to Broadway to look for their big break. For a beginner in the news business, the big break is more likely to be found far from the big cities. There aren't as many bright lights, but there are more openings. Besides, the beginning work will be far more satisfying. Even the beginner who lucks into a job on a metropolitan daily is in for a time of apprenticeship, one cut above copyboy, doing the least demanding jobs in the place. Better to be covering bigger stories in a smaller place.

Finding the right smaller place is a challenge, but a reporter ought to be able to meet it. Check the newspaper directories and write to editors. The most receptive may be the ones closest to home; you may not know the business, but at least you know the territory. The search can be as simple as looking in the help-wanted advertisements in trade publications like *Editor & Publisher.*

Last time the Census Bureau checked, more than 48,000 Americans were working as reporters or editors. Twenty-two thousand of them were women. That's a good number to keep in mind when the search gets discouraging.

Whether you want a career in broadcast or print journalism, your best bet is to start in print. It is a better way of continuing your education.

Newspaper deadlines require an editorial staff, and an editorial staff represents, for a beginning reporter, a graduate school. There are colleagues who will help with writing; there is a copy desk which will trim, rewrite and edit; there is an editor who will complain.

All of that is a necessary part of the learning process, done in real time, against real deadlines, for real money in a paycheck. There is no substitute.

Newspapers and magazines worry more about words than local radio and television stations, which have their own requirements for speed and performance. Words are basic, and the place to learn to use them, to be afraid of them, to respect them, to worry about them, to have fun with them, is in print.

Radio and television, of necessity, place emphasis on many skills: editing of audio or video tape, on-camera delivery, speaking rather than writing. Good journalists have come out of that background, but in too many cases these people have had to learn about words in midcareer. Sometimes, even among successful broadcast journalists, it shows. Better to start with writing.

It takes time to become a competent reporter and writer. On newspapers and magazines, reporting and writing skills can be learned without involvement in the technicalities of editing, makeup and printing. In radio and television, the newcomer usually must cope with the technology, and this diminishes the time available for writing and reporting.

Once the basics are habit, there is ample time to decide whether your career should be in print or in broadcasting, in features or in hard news, in radio or in television. Or, for that matter, in some other line of work.

The techniques of the various media come quickly and easily, once the fundamentals of journalism are established.

Besides, a competent print reporter can get a job in radio or television more easily than a TV reporter can move to a newspaper. Starting in print opens more career options.

Now, how do you start in print? Simple. You want to be a reporter, so be one. Reporters check contacts. Okay, your father's second cousin works in Tacoma and knows people at the newspaper.

But he writes to say there are no jobs there. One of your teachers knows the editor of the local paper. No jobs there, either. You make the rounds in your home territory, and, again, there are no jobs. What then?

Don't give up. It takes time. You've been waiting for years to start your career, and if it is worth what you think it is, it's worth working for, patiently.

A. J. Liebling once hired a man to walk up and down in front of a newspaper wearing a signboard which read: "Hire Joe Liebling." Not a bad stunt, but when Liebling saw the paper's editor after several days of sidewalk advertising, he discovered that the editor had never seen the sign, because he came and went through the back door.

Imagination and inventiveness are, after all, part of what you're selling. Editors want reporters who can think fast and work the angles.

Again, check the directories. *Editor & Publisher* issues an annual volume listing every paper in the country, with address, telephone number, and the names and titles of the editors and other top people.

Write to them, but do some research first. Find out something about the paper and the people who run it. Address them by title—and get it right. Editors do not hire reporters on the basis of letters that begin: "To Whom It May Concern." Or: "To The Editor." Or any variation thereof. Or who misspell their names.

You are asking somebody to pay you a salary to get information and write it into readable news stories. If you can't get information about the place you want to work, and write a readable letter, forget it.

Talk with as many people as you can, and write to more. Tell the editor that even if there is no job on his staff, you'd like a few minutes with him when it's convenient, because you'd profit from the advice such a titan of journalism could offer a beginner. Editors are not immune to flattery. Nor are Washington bureau chiefs or network commentators.

So you've done all that, to no avail.

If you can't get a hard-news job, sign up with an organization that will put you in contact with hard-news people. Ask one of your local politicians if you can help out in press relations. See if a local charity needs help. If there's a restaurant or bar where reporters gather, go there. Reporters love to talk.

MEARS: When you go through life as a reporter, it seems as though half the people you meet used to be reporters themselves. Or at least say they were. And that anybody who didn't used to be wants to be. I was in a particularly seamy café on the North Beach strip in San Francisco one time with some other political reporters. We started chatting with one of the dancers. Turned out she was working her way through journalism school, and wanted to know how to get a job when she graduated. Or at least that's what she said.

A friend of mine hired the cocktail waitress at a bar he used to frequent. She turned out to be a good newswoman and left the print side to take one of those high-priced New York jobs you television people have.

It is easier to get a job if you have a job. Being employed at just about anything changes your attitude and makes you more attractive to those who might hire you. Jobs in journalism aren't available every day, and if you are able to assure an editor that you're not idle and about to die of hunger, it improves the odds.

Education is vital. A journalism school can open the way to a beginner's job, because it provides some practical experience and contacts.

But don't place too much emphasis on practical techniques at the expense of general education. It may sound appealing to take courses in photography, makeup, advertising and video-tape editing, but if they take too much time from history, science or economics, a young journalist can end up with a lot of technical knowledge and nothing to say.

The work of journalism is the observation of humans. The observation of humans is called the humanities. The more you can learn about what humans have done and said, where they've been and what they believe, the better journalist you'll be.

The classics can be of direct, practical help to someone who wants to write news. Herodotus, in ancient Greece, was perhaps the world's first travel writer. Thucydides was a great war correspondent. Jonathan Swift was a marvelous columnist. Shakespeare could say more with fewer words than almost anybody.

Philosophy, history, political science and economics are of special value in the training of a journalist.

Take them all in, and find a specialty too. It may not turn

out to be your journalistic specialty, but a political reporter who majored in economics is one whose education will serve him well. Science specialists are in demand in this age of technology, and while that's not a beginning job, the reporter with a degree in that area will have an advantage later on, when the science writer quits and the editor needs a new one quickly. Besides, most people who want to report and write for a living cannot add, subtract, or figure out why computers do what they do. If you write well, understand science and technology, and chew gum at the same time, you've got a winning combination.

Language training is valuable, for its practical application and because it can make you a better writer. You may never be a foreign correspondent, may not want to be, but a reporter fluent in Spanish will be an asset to news organizations in many American cities with large Hispanic populations. And if you want to work abroad, foreign correspondents nowadays know the language or they don't get the assignment.

CHANCELLOR: I spent some years in Europe and the Soviet Union as a foreign correspondent. I had some French and some very limited Russian, plus enough German to get around, but in Italy, Scandinavia and places like Yugoslavia, I relied on what might be called correspondent's pidgin. Every night I would spend time with a dictionary or phrase book, writing down the things I would absolutely have to say the next day, and writing them in the simplest possible way. I used infinitives for most of my verb forms. It's a lot easier to say "to go" to a taxi driver than it is to say, "I would like to go." Translators are essential when you can't speak the language, but you can't be with them all the time, and a list of essential words on a card you can hold in your hand can save your life.

There will always be American correspondents overseas, but the number has been decreasing. One study in 1963 counted 515 full-time Americans working overseas. In 1975, the Overseas

Press Club listed 429. That means more competition for fewer jobs, and if you want one of them, you'll have to know the language.

MEARS: I never got past English, and wish I had. It has always seemed to me that a writer who was fluent in a second language would have extra options in choosing words and constructing phrases. The more ways there are to say something, the more likely it is that you'll say it readably and well.

So I think another language would have been useful, even though I had no interest in becoming a foreign correspondent. I was always too fascinated by what was going on here, in government and politics. It would be nice and tidy to say that is how political reporting became my specialty, but it isn't. It happened because Barry Goldwater ran into my boss at a cocktail party in 1963 and complained that AP wasn't paying enough attention to the presidential campaign he was starting at the time. The boss agreed and sent me out to cover him. All of a sudden I was a political reporter. I'm glad Barry was at that party.

For all the specialization in modern newswriting, the new reporter on the small paper is going to be a generalist, covering a little of everything. There's likely to be an assignment at city hall one day, an obit to be handled when you get back, and a school board meeting to cover after that. You'll get used to checking police headquarters to get the accident and crime reports for tomorrow's paper. And you'll get a taste of two specialties that eventually come to be full-time jobs for some reporters: sports and business news.

Every paper has a sports section; the big ones have a separate business section too.

Business news is a growth industry. There is more financial and business reporting in today's newspapers than ever before, because there is more interest in the subject. What once was a dusty corner of the operation, producing copy that read suspiciously like corporate handouts, has become a showcase section in many dailies.

It is a difficult subject to handle well and readably. Some of the people who do it still write in technical language, but the best business writers are translators, taking the arcane language of the corporate world and rendering it into understandable prose.

The reporting has changed too. Corporate America is no longer treated as a community immune from inquiry and investigation. It is being probed and questioned, often to the irritation of businessmen, who liked the old style better.

It's a promising area for a young reporter whose interests tend that way. If those *are* your interests, work to develop them. When there's a business story to be written, volunteer. You won't be covering the takeover wars of corporate giants, but the story of a local firm that is expanding, or hiring, or adding a new line—or folding—is more important to the readers you'll be serving anyhow. Give those readers some financial reporting they wouldn't get without you.

They'll be better informed, and you'll be better prepared when a job comes open on the business news staff at the big city paper you'd like to join. They want experience, and you'll have it to offer.

But don't kid yourself into thinking that a couple of good stories about local business will get you out of checking the cops for accident reports.

Count on covering some sports too, whether you like sports or not. It goes with the territory when you're a newcomer, general-assignment reporter on a paper with a small staff. Don't plan on the Super Bowl or the World Series. Figure on high school basketball, down toward the end of the season, when the game is important enough for the editor to send a reporter instead of using a stringer who calls in the score and some detail for a story.

It isn't even minor-league stuff, but—here comes that word again—it's valuable experience. The crowd is small and the players are kids instead of high-priced superstars. But the game is the same game they play at Madison Square Garden. You can learn at least as much, and maybe more, writing about the game in the high school gym. If you want to make it your line of work, that's the way to get there. Athletes practice every day, and good sportswriters do too.

It is not the heaviest line of work in journalism, and that may help to explain why sportswriting has produced some of the finest writers in the business. James Reston was a sportswriter early in the career that made him one of the most influential of Washington newsmen. Ernest Hemingway, Damon Runyon, Quentin Reynolds and Paul Gallico all wrote sports before they became novelists. Red Smith (nobody called him Walter) was a sportswriter until he died, and no newsman wrote better.

It may be that sportswriters, grown men paid to write about games, learn not to take themselves too seriously. Some of their colleagues in more solemn lines of inquiry take themselves very seriously, and produce coagulated copy as a result. Because sportswriters are writing about diversions, not about life and death, they have a freedom of expression other newswriters do not.

Besides, since the game is always the same—nine innings or until one side wins, 162 times a year in the major leagues—sportswriters have to exert more than ordinary effort to avoid writing the same story over and over again. They have to look for color and change, and they have to find a different way to tell the story.

Many of them don't succeed. They lapse into clichés, stringing them together until the story is done. AP once sent out a note asking sports editors to list the clichés they found most offensive, the idea being to get them out of the copy. One sports editor refused to reply, saying he wasn't sending his clichés to a wire service. "Let them get their own clichés."

Sportswriting is a difficult specialty to crack, because so many reporters want to do it, or at least think so for a while. Whether it's your goal or not, read the sports page for the writing. There is a lot to be learned there, from people who earn their living by getting the facts straight and making the reading enjoyable.

It isn't easy to do those two things. It isn't easy to get a start in the news business, nor is it easy to be good at it.

But the effort is worth making.

The late Frank Graham, the sports columnist, once observed that journalism will kill you, but it'll keep you alive in the meantime.

It is difficult work, often frustrating, frequently exhausting, not the way to get rich. Every slip is out there in print or public view, to draw scorn, wrath—or lawsuits. Somehow, it seems, the good, solid stories seldom draw the same attention.

It also is exciting, fascinating, constantly challenging and changing work. The people who do it are a fraternity. They understand each other as no outsider can. They talk in a kind of verbal shorthand about what they do, about their stories, their subjects, their editors, their professional frustrations. Sometimes the latter two are synonymous.

And no reporter in a strange city ever is farther from a friend than the distance to the local newspaper office, or the bar where the press hangs out.

Newspeople spend a lot of their time waiting, for the telephone call to be answered or the meeting to end or the senator to come out of hiding in his office.

When those are crucial elements of a story, there's nothing to do but wait, sometimes in vain. The governor walks by and won't say a word. The phone call is not returned. The politician who was just indicted slips out of the courthouse by the side door.

Perhaps because there's so much waiting time, and because they write stories for a living, newspeople tell a lot of inside stories. Topics vary, but expense-account yarns are among the favorites.

It is told that a sportswriter assigned to cover the old New York Giants used to charge his newspaper for cab fares to and from the ball park whenever the team played in Pittsburgh. One summer, an expense account was returned with a note from the auditor. It is supposed to have said: "I went to Pittsburgh on my vacation and the ball park is right across the street from the hotel." The sportswriter is said to have replied: "Only an auditor would go to Pittsburgh on his vacation."

Reporters get to go places and see things other people don't. Some even get paid to go to the World Series. Some breeze in and out of town in political motorcades, and never mind the rush hour. They are allowed up close, behind the police lines, to watch and ask questions.

Sometimes they get carried away.

Once, when a political campaign paused for a half day at an amusement park in California, reporter-author Theodore H. White organized a trip to the fun house. A half-dozen reporters headed for the ticket office, only to find a long line. Teddy White wasn't stalled. He pulled out his press card, walked to the head of the line, said, "National press," and bought tickets.

This did not please the people waiting in line. They didn't see why the national press should get priority treatment at the fun house.

But perhaps it was fitting.

It's a serious business, done best by people who don't take themselves too seriously.

They wind up watching history happen, and they are paid to be there, and to write down what they have seen and heard. Then they get to tell everyone else about it.

And then they do it again. For the job has to do with tomorrow. Today's story may have been a masterpiece, a prize-winner. It may have been a bust. Either way, it won't last, because the news business is about tomorrow. And no one in it is any better than what they will do tomorrow.